The Life of Jesus Christ

The Life of
JESUS CHRIST

by W. Norman Pittenger, S.T.D.

FRANKLIN WATTS, INC.
575 Lexington Avenue
New York, N.Y. 10022

Contents

Author's Note

There can be no doubt that among the "immortals"
—men and women whom we can never forget and
about whom every educated person should be informed
—Jesus is an extraordinary figure. To a Christian
believer, this may seem an almost startling understate-
ment, for he regards Jesus not only as a historical figure
but also as the Lord, whom he follows and reveres as
a truly divine being. The author of this book is himself a Christian believer and shares the faith of Christians in Jesus. But he is convinced that one need not
necessarily share that faith to learn about the Man of
Nazareth. On the contrary, everybody can and should
know about Jesus, and understand him in the light of
the best modern scholarship. And those who, like the

author, are Christian believers have nothing whatever to fear from such a scholarly approach. Many people will welcome just such a study as this book attempts, whether or not they call themselves Christians. Perhaps some readers, once they have learned what can be known and said about Jesus, may seriously consider the claims that Christians make for Jesus as one who is to be followed, and as one who may truly be described as divine.

The purpose of this book is *not* to make converts to Christianity but to present facts based on the best scholarship of our day. Of course, in such a book as this, one cannot write with the experts always in mind. The author can only hope that what they have to tell us will be faithfully reported. The reader, in turn, will be required to make his own contribution as he goes through these pages. Jesus of Nazareth is not a subject that can be written about or read about as if one were simply concerned with a good story or a novel. The material in question is too complicated and the subject too important for that kind of approach either by the writer or the reader.

The reader therefore is urged to study the book with care and with a concentrated effort of attention. He should also read the four gospels. If he wishes to pursue the subject further, there is an appended list of suggested reading. The books that are mentioned are acknowledged as important and scholarly works by those who are expert in the field.

In this book the approach to the central figure is of necessity different from that taken in most other biographical studies. The reason is that both the sources that must be used and the way they must be approached are different from those appropriate to other "immortal" biographies. I would have been thoroughly dishonest if I had tried to write a "biography" of Jesus as one might write a biography of Abraham Lincoln or of Julius Caesar. Such a biography cannot be written of Jesus, for he appears as a unique figure in history. I have tried to show that one must begin with an account of the historical background and setting—the context—in which Jesus appears; and then describe the kind of information we have about him and how it will be used. Unless this is done, the succeeding chapters will be wrongly interpreted and open to serious misunderstanding.

Translations in this book are from the King James Bible or the author's own translations from Greek.

It remains to say that I am indebted to so many other scholars that I cannot even begin to mention their names. But I wish especially to thank former colleagues at the General Theological Seminary in New York and present colleagues at Cambridge University in England. Their assistance in answering my questions, the sharing of their expert knowledge in various fields, together with their readiness to refer me to books and essays, have been most helpful in preparing this volume.

W. N. P.

King's College
Cambridge, England

The Life of Jesus Christ

Prologue

Someone has said that history is made by its great personalities. Most of us are born, live for a certain number of years, die, and are eventually forgotten. But some men and women are not forgotten; the impact they make on the world is so great that they are always remembered. There are not many such people—perhaps only a few hundred—but they have changed the world.

Among those great personalities, no one has done more to mold our world than a young Jewish artisan named Jesus. For millions of people during the past two thousand years, and for countless other millions today, this Jesus is more than just an important man. To them, he is the disclosure of the character of God, the clue to the meaning that they find in human life. But even for people who do not share this belief in Jesus, his importance is immense. He is a force that everyone must somehow or other come to terms with.

If you stop to think about it, this is a surprising fact. After all, in his own day, Jesus was an obscure man, living in a part of the world that had little to do with the great affairs of nations. He was born of humble parents and he spent his entire life within a tiny land called Palestine. He was killed at an early age—when he was in his thirties—and there are no records about him such as those usually written about other world figures. He himself did not write any books. Indeed, we know of only one instance of his writing anything at all. That was when he "wrote on the ground," as he was talking with a poor woman who was being taunted by some self-righteous men. (The story can be found in John's Gospel in the New Testament, Chapter 8, verses 3 to 11.) He did not lead an army nor did he occupy any place of authority in government. He was an artisan, or as translations of the Greek of the New Testament say, "a carpenter." To all appearances he was not the sort of person usually regarded as a great figure in history.

Yet of that greatness there is no doubt. The purpose of this book is to explain why and how Jesus came to occupy the place in history that all succeeding ages have given him. There are, however, three points that should be remembered about Jesus and his significance.

First is the fact that Jesus changed the recording of history. The way in which we refer to time is an indication of this. We live in the era called "A.D." which means *anno Domini*, the Latin for "in the year of the Lord." The "Lord" in that phrase refers to Jesus. We speak of the period before Jesus as "B.C.," which means "before Christ." That turning point in history, made by a man in Palestine some two thousand years ago, is so important that it has affected even our own time scheme. Understandably, thoughtful persons will want to know about the man responsible for this dramatic change.

They will also wonder why Jesus should have affected our way of giving dates. The answer is that within a very short time after his death, Jesus came to have a remarkable place in the thoughts and actions of the people who lived near the Mediterranean Sea. They believed that Jesus disclosed the character of God, and that only through Jesus could there be a right relationship between God and man. So it was inevitable that men eventually decided to date events as happening before, or as happening after, that decisive time when Jesus appeared on earth.

Second, what Jesus said has vital meaning for the world. His teaching is summed up in what has been called the "Golden Rule," which tells us that we should always do to others what we want to have done to ourselves. But more important than the "rule" itself is how Jesus explained and interpreted its meaning. He said that the only way men and women can live together in the world is by showing an understanding, sympathetic, and loving spirit in all their human relationships. This means that they are also to concern themselves with justice, for justice between men and nations is one way in which genuine love manifests itself. W. H. Auden, a modern poet, has phrased this idea in unforgettable words: "We must love one another, or die." We know this to be true only too well. For we live in a world where we are all dependent upon each other, and where what happens ten thousand miles away may greatly affect us at home. That is why the statesmen of the world, however unwillingly, are being forced to come to some understanding so that an enduring peace among the nations can be established. Every war, and every threat of war; every famine in any land, however remote; every act of injustice or segregation of race from race or class from class—all of these conditions we now know are intolerable and destructive. Jesus knew all this and said all this two thousand years ago. He made it clear that unless we learn to love one another, we shall indeed die.

If he had done nothing else, the fact that he did see and say this would have been sufficient to give him contemporary importance. No longer is it just a matter of "religion," as if his teaching about love had to do only with men's private lives. It is now a matter of absolute urgency. Nobody can doubt this today.

The third point to remember is that Jesus not only expressed these ideas, he lived them out in his own experience. Had Jesus been nothing more than a great teacher, he might have been forgotten. But because he lived out, in actual relations with other people, what he declared to be the truth, he is the demonstration of his own ideas. What he said, that he did. His importance in history is that of an enacted truth, not a truth that people only talk about. Jesus was ready to die for what he knew to be true. And so he is the pattern on which men and women have tried to model their lives. Although most of those who have tried to follow the example of Jesus have been only partially successful, they continue to believe in his truths, and are spurred to stronger efforts to put them into practice.

In human history, people have followed many leaders—daring conquerors, dictators, cheats, and clever manipulators. They may have appeared successful for a time. But in the long run we remember them with contempt and disgust, and we fear the results of their actions. Hitler and Napoleon and men with grasping power have caused terrible destruction. To follow their example leads only to further destruction and perhaps even to the annihilation of life on this planet. There is only one real option before us—to love one another or die. That is the way the grain of the universe runs. To go against that grain is only to invite disaster for ourselves and others.

Christians believe that Jesus is not only the most remarkable man who ever lived. They also believe that he embodies the truth about everything in human life and in the whole world. That truth reveals God as "pure unbounded love." And that God who is love, and who is everywhere, is also in the nature of His human children. To the Christian, this divine love reaches its supreme expression in the person of the poor artisan who lived in Palestine two thousand years ago. For the believer, the Man of Nazareth is Master and Lord.

There are many who do not accept this faith in Jesus. Yet Jesus still remains the centrally important person in our history, for he taught and lived the truth about human life and the world. The approach, therefore, to this study of Jesus is not that of the evangelist trying to convert others. It is an attempt to explain why this Man of Nazareth has the place in history that the ages have given him.

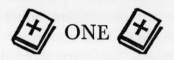

ONE

JESUS' BACKGROUND

Ralph Waldo Emerson, the famous New England essayist of the nineteenth century, once said of Jesus of Nazareth, that "his name is not so much written as ploughed into history." As Emerson saw it, Jesus' name—and this means his life expressed in words and actions—stands for more than just an incident in the past. The great Indian patriot Gandhi was not a Christian, but a practicing Hindu. Yet Gandhi insisted that Jesus was a man so important in the history of the world and so significant in his own right, that all Indians should know about him, respect him, and find a place for him in their scheme of things.

Jesus cannot be understood unless we know something about the people who went before him and lived with him in the little Near Eastern country where he spent his life. In fact, it is impossible really to understand anybody without understanding the world in which he lived. To find out what made Abraham Lincoln great, you must first learn about the history and thoughts of the United States before he was born. Studying the background of his life, you get some idea of the problems that faced not only Lincoln the man but also the country that he served. You soon begin to appreciate the influence he exerted during his lifetime and how he was regarded by others in the years that followed. For nobody is separate from his surroundings. Everybody lives at a particular time, in a particular place, and has a particular background. This means that everybody in one way or another affects or is affected by other people—even if they are only his family and friends.

And so, to understand Jesus we should have some knowledge of the history of the Jewish people and where they lived. For Jesus was a Jew of the first century, who lived, as most Jews did then, in Palestine.

What sort of place was Palestine in the first century? It was a small country about the size of the state of Vermont. Lying on the shores of the Mediterranean Sea, Palestine occupied part of the section of Asia now called the Near East. It was a beautiful, hilly, even mountainous land. It also had dusty deserts, a large salt lake named the Dead Sea, and areas that were extremely arid, for much of Palestine lay below sea level.

10

There were also high points of land, some of them several thousand feet above sea level. One of these rises, Mount Lebanon, was snow-covered for most of the year. Although today much of the Palestine area is treeless and a good deal of it without rich vegetation, in earlier days it was fairly well wooded and many sections were extremely fertile. The valley through which the river Jordan flows, connecting the freshwater Lake of Galilee with the Dead Sea, was especially lush and green.

Palestine was well populated, with its large capital city of Jerusalem on a hilltop, and with many towns and villages numbering hundreds or thousands of inhabitants. The population was made up of a mixture of people. While the majority were of Jewish descent, there were people who infiltrated from other lands. In some parts, such as Samaria to the north, considerable intermarriage had produced a number of people of mixed ancestry. On the coast of the Mediterranean there was still another mixture of people. Here the older Phoenicians had had their home. And to the east across the Jordan, there was the desert where Semitic Bedouins lived, much as do the present-day nomadic Arabs who have no settled dwellings. At the time of Jesus there was also considerable regional spirit, for the many Jewish inhabitants of the south, with their center in Jerusalem, held a different outlook from those in Galilee, farther to the north.

11

The whole area was governed by the Romans, who some time earlier had conquered the country and occupied its capital. Through governors sent from Rome, they exercised general control over the people, although in some sections they used local rulers as their agents. There was much economic deprivation, not only because the country was relatively poor but also because of the heavy taxes that Rome imposed. Roman soldiers were stationed at many places throughout the land to keep order. In Jerusalem itself there was a substantial force ready to put down a possible revolt, and at all times acting as the military support of the resident Roman governor.

From Jerusalem, the Great Sanhedrin, or supreme court of the Jews, more or less governed the central area of the country, in uneasy collaboration with the Roman rulers. In religious matters, of course, the Sanhedrin was supreme. Its membership was made up principally of representatives of old high-priestly families, the Sadducees, whose chief interest seems to have been the preservation of the status quo, or keeping things as they were. In each town in Palestine there were one or more synagogues, or places of worship and teaching. Each of these had its own council, although in most places these councils looked to the Great Sanhedrin for guidance. Because Judaism was so largely a "religion of the book," based on what we today call the Old Testament, the Jews were surprisingly literate. The synagogue schools ensured that they were instructed in the traditional sacred writings, and all the people were aware of their history as a nation and were proud of their position as a "chosen people."

Judaism at this time included a variety of sects, or particular groups, who each had their own special way of interpreting the Jewish religion and applying it to the issues of the day. In addition to the Sadducees, of established position and conservative tendencies, the Pharisees were also prominent both in Jerusalem and other parts of the country. The Pharisees, often mistakenly thought of as being hypocritical and petty, were actually highly conscientious, loyal, and devout Jews. They firmly believed that it was necessary to relate the inherited Jewish faith to the actual situation of the people. The Pharisees differed from the Sadducees, and recognized the need for developing the traditional Jewish teachings.

They fully accepted the ancient Law of Moses, but by their interpretations of that law they tried to make it effective in their own time. For this purpose, they referred to an enormous amount of interpretation made by teachers in the past. This way of dealing with old beliefs and practices is somewhat like the way in which the United States Supreme Court "interprets the Constitution." The court adapts the Constitution's meaning to changing conditions, and for this purpose it uses the growing body of interpretation made both by the Court itself and by lower courts in earlier days of the nation's history.

There were also in Palestine groups of Jews called Zealots, who were intense in their belief that the Jewish people and their religion were specially chosen and directed by God. These patriots adopted a violently antagonistic attitude toward the Roman rulers controlling the land.

The existence of the Essenes, another sect of Jews living in the Palestine area, was confirmed in 1947, with the discovery of the Dead Sea Scrolls. The scrolls, along with the ruins of communities, were uncovered in Qumrân, near the Dead Sea. The story of the discoveries and excavations makes exciting reading. The existence of the Essenes and related groups had always been known to scholars, for in early writings a good deal had been said about these people. Although many Essenes had withdrawn from ordinary Jewish life and had established their own settlements in isolated places, their ideas had penetrated the Jewish thinking of the time. Some scholars have associated John the Baptist with the Essenes, and many of the sayings of Jesus himself show familiarity with elements of Essene teaching.

Any study of Jewish religious history presents many difficult problems of interpretation and fact, but some points are generally agreed upon among scholars.

It was the conviction of the Jews that they were a

people "chosen by God." This belief had its roots in their past history and especially in the experience they had known as a people. From their earliest days the Jews believed that they alone had been in the care of the God whom they called Yahweh. (In many English versions of the Bible this name is also translated as "Jehovah.") Yahweh was originally a god of the storm, revealed in earthquakes, thunder and lightning, and other then inexplicable events. It is easy to understand how a seminomadic people would be awed by such natural occurrences. During these extraordinary events they would feel themselves in the presence of a superhuman power that was both fierce and wonderful. This sense of more-than-human power increased as the people came to recognize that their God of power was also the God of righteousness, justice, and mercy; the God who was always "faithful," meaning that His actions, however unpredictable, were consistent with His purpose.

The first figure in Jewish history who "moralized" the concept, or idea, of Yahweh, the God of storm and earthquake, was the prophet Moses. It was Moses who led the Jews out of their slavery in Egypt. It was Moses who insisted that the God whom they worshiped had chosen the Jews as His people and had disclosed His righteous character to them. God had chosen them—He had brought them out of Egypt under the leadership of His servant Moses. And He had revealed His will for righteousness through Moses, who had received the Ten Commandments, the moral code of justice that was to be observed among men.

Historically, the Ten Commandments probably reflected the tribal customs that had developed among the Jews, and were a Jewish version of moral laws already being established in those parts of the world. What is significant, however, is that, under Moses and those who followed him, the Jews came to believe firmly that these regulations were the will of the God who had made the Jews His very own people. He had given them a "law which cannot be broken" so that they might continue to be His people, enact His will, and represent Him among the nations of the earth.

In Moses' time, Judaism had probably not reached "monotheism," or the belief in only one God. But it had reached the stage of "henotheism," meaning that there was only one God (for the Jews), though others might worship many "gods." Certainly Judaism was "momentarily monotheistic," for on the occasions when the Jews felt themselves most truly in God's presence, their God was in fact the only "god" who mattered.

After the Jews entered Canaan, or Palestine, they came to regard this country as the land of Israel, the Holy Land given them by God. They were convinced that the God who had brought them from Egypt under Moses had also led them, under successors of Moses, into a country that was to be theirs forever. But contact with the people already settled in the land brought new difficulties, for these people worshiped local deities. To preserve the integrity of their inherited faith, the Israelites "assimilated" the local deities to Yahweh himself. They came to regard the fertility cults and other local beliefs as all part of Yahweh's continuing care for His human children. So the God who had been seen in the unusual events of nature was now also seen as the God who had power over life's ordinary affairs. This change of viewpoint was not easy to make, for there was always the temptation to regard Yahweh as just another one of the local deities. This danger was averted by the watchfulness of the prophets of early Israel, such as Amos and Hosea, and the less-well-documented figures of Elijah and Elisha.

It was the prophets of Israel who further developed the conception of God. For the Jews, a prophet was not someone who foretold the future but one who was impelled by some strong inner urge to speak what he took to be God's will. He was believed to be a man guided by God, and chosen as the mouthpiece for God. The prophets explained God's nature and purpose, and showed the people the way to true religious action.

In early Israel, the prophet Hosea was an important figure. It was Hosea who first began to teach his fellow Jews that the God who was powerful and righteous was also merciful and loving toward His chosen people.

17

No matter how much the Israelites might sin by violating God's commandments, God would forgive them and still care for them, Hosea declared. God's love was like the love of a husband for his faithless wife whom he has forgiven. God's love was also like that of a loving father, and "like as a father pitieth his own children," so God was loving and merciful. But He was not an easy God to please. He expected and demanded obedience to His will. His love was real but it was also stern.

It is Isaiah who is generally considered to be the greatest of the Jewish prophets in the Old Testament. He expounded what today we call God's "transcendence," as well as God's righteousness and His care for His people. Transcendence here refers to God as being exalted and glorious. He rules over all the universe, and is never simply identified with human affairs or with the world of nature. Isaiah proclaimed God to be the Holy One of Israel, who required holiness in His chosen people. In the Old Testament, holiness does not mean simply goodness or virtue. Primarily, holiness means the capacity to be one's self, so that one preserves his selfhood and integrity in relations with others. When applied to God, holiness also means that He puts us in great awe, at the same time attracting us to Himself by His wonder and glory. For Isaiah, God was always and unchangeably *God*, in whose presence men must worship and adore, while they were also

18

drawn to Him in the urgent desire to know Him as He always knew them.

Isaiah was also the first clear exponent of what we call ethical monotheism. The God known to the Jews was the one God; there could only be one God who controlled nature and the events in history. Everything was dependent upon Him for He had created the world and all that was in it. And He was perfectly righteous, or "ethical." He cared for His people and would never desert them. Furthermore, not only did He care for Israel, He cared for the whole world, and for everyone in it, no matter the nation or race. His purpose was being worked out in the affairs of men, even when they did not recognize Him as God. The unique privilege of the Jews as the chosen people was not that God looked after them only, but that they had been given the secret of His character and of His will. Their job was to serve God in such a way that other nations and people would also come to know God and worship Him.

In addition to the messages of Isaiah another crucial religious theme began to emerge in the writings of the Jews. God not only loved all nations, He also loved individual men. He cared for all men; He cared for each man. For example, the prophet Jeremiah, in the Old Testament, stressed the tenderness of God and His willingness to suffer with His children. God was identified with His world and shared in its anguish. Yet in sharing in suffering, God was not overcome by it. Precisely because God was transcendent and holy, He was able to take suffering to Himself and achieve victory over it. This kind of understanding of God attained by Jeremiah, in the times before Christ, strongly suggests the beliefs arrived at by Christians, especially Paul and John in the New Testament. They discovered God's identification with men in the man Jesus, and in what they believed to be Jesus' triumph. They saw the victory of God Himself over both suffering and death.

Soon a central idea about God became prominent in all of the later writings of the Jewish religious world, and was eventually taken into the Christian interpretation of Jesus. It was the belief in "the kingdom of God," or "God's kingly or sovereign rule in His world."

Of course, the Jews always believed that God ruled the world. He had created it, and nothing was or could be beyond His control. But His rule was not accepted and recognized everywhere, and as a result, much had gone wrong with things in the world. It was necessary that evil and wickedness should be exterminated and God's sovereignty expressed in all the affairs of men. This was especially important for the Jews to believe. In their history the very land that they said God had given them was conquered by the Assyrians, and the Jews became a subject people. Many of them were taken away as captives to the Tigris-Euphrates area while those left in Palestine were under severe oppression. Even when they received a certain amount of self-government under King Cyrus, who conquered the Assyrian-Babylonian empire, the Jews never really felt secure. Later, when the Syrian-Grecian successors of Alexander the Great occupied the land and even dared to interfere with their worship, the Jews believed themselves to be almost deserted by their God. But a group of leaders called the Maccabeans reasserted Jewish self-rule, and once again it seemed that God had come to the aid of the Jews. Within a fairly short time, however, Palestine was conquered once again, this time by the Romans. Once more the Jews were a subject people. And once again, they were sure that God would visibly manifest His sovereign rule.

Against this background rose the belief that the God who had chosen the Jews as His people would also "redeem" them. He would come to save them from their enemies. And He would establish a kingdom in which He—God—would be ruler, and they—His people—would live in peace and security. For some Jews this meant terrible cosmic occurrences, with strange signs in the heavens and a war upon earth. A kingly representative of God would then appear and establish Jerusalem as the center of the world. Others accepted and taught a more peaceful idea of the "coming of the kingdom." But however the kingdom was to be established, the conviction was widespread that one day, and perhaps very soon, there would be a visible sign of divine power. The God whom the Jews worshiped would restore their freedom and give them a position of supremacy among the nations of the earth. This was their great national expectation—although some Jews, like the Sadducees, seemed content to accept foreign rule as long as they were allowed to continue Temple worship in Jerusalem and to maintain their traditional religious customs.

The religious life of the Jew and all of his secular life as well (if he were faithful to the traditions of his people) found their center in devoted obedience to what was regarded as the divinely approved Law, or the Torah. This was a body of legal codes that provided the Jews with guidance in every moral, civil, or religious situation that might arise. The Jews worshiped both in community synagogues and in the great Temple in Jerusalem. Here daily sacrifices prescribed in the Law were carried on by the Temple priesthood. These sacrifices included the regular offering of lambs on behalf of the people. There were also other ceremonies associated with the holy days and the seasonal festivals. Every Jew wanted to visit Jerusalem at least once in his lifetime, and great pilgrimages brought thousands to the city every year. The Temple rites, performed according to the Law, served to bind together all the Jewish people, those in the homeland and those elsewhere in the Roman Empire, who were called "the dispersion."

Although worship in the Temple was important, in actual practice it was the synagogue in each community, large or small, that provided the true religious center for the Jew during most of his life. The synagogue was a combination school and place of worship. On Saturday of each week, the holy day called the Sabbath, a service was attended by the entire membership. Regular weekday services were also held for the faithful. At the village school, located in the synagogue building, it was the duty of every Israelite, if at all possible, to learn to read the sacred books of the Law. At least it was his duty to be present to hear the Law read week-by-week, with comments from the specially trained rabbi, or exponent of the Law.

The faithful Jew tried to practice the precepts laid down in the Law, and he was helped to do this by the rabbi's explanations. These leaders have been described as a kind of "unofficial clergy." They were not priests, for the priestly clan was in the Jerusalem Temple. The rabbis were not members of a special caste that separated them from the rest of the chosen people. They were specially trained, of course, but religion for the Jew was never a matter of a distinctive priestly caste. Although only a priest could give a blessing or offer the Temple sacrifices, every Jew was by birth a member of a nation that was regarded as being priestly in the broadest sense. For this reason every pious Jew had an immediate and lively interest in religious matters.

However, there were many Jews who, through ignorance, carelessness, or sheer necessity, could not or did not fully practice the rituals of Jewish piety. To a greater or lesser degree these people followed the general line of Jewish customs, since they could not live among their fellows without doing so. Yet they had their own simple piety. In much surviving literature they are not very sympathetically portrayed, for among the leaders of the people they were usually regarded as those who did not follow the Law, and hence were thought of as second-class citizens.

Many scholars think that the quiet type of religion suggested in the first chapters of Luke's Gospel represents the position of these Jews. Most likely Jesus made a very special appeal to this kind of person. Much of official Judaism was probably too complicated for these people to follow. The straightforward, simple, and uncomplicated teachings of Jesus seemed to speak more directly to them.

In sum, these were the religious beliefs and attitudes in Palestine at the time when Jesus was born. The Jewish religion was highly ethical in its teaching. Worship in the Temple and in the synagogue was important and necessary. In daily life that religion would be expressed by a righteous, godly, morally responsible, and obedient observance of God's revealed holy will.

There was a general acceptance of belief in one God, who had created the world and who was the supreme ruler of all things. This God was regarded as being supremely "a person," and in His dealings with men He showed himself in personal ways. He was a righteous God who would not tolerate anything that was unjust. He was good, pure, and holy. Anything that was evil, impure, or profane was an abomination to Him. He was to be worshiped as the "high and lofty One that inhabiteth eternity," but He was also "nigh unto those who are of a humble and contrite spirit."

He was the Father of His people Israel. Because He had chosen Israel as His people, He demanded that they be exemplary in fulfilling His will, which He had revealed to them in the divine Law and, above all, in the Ten Commandments. He would judge His people by their loyalty or disloyalty to that will. And He would judge all nations and all men by their fulfillment of that will. Through Noah and the Flood, God had revealed His power in a very real sense to all people, but the people of Israel had special obligations that they were expected to obey faithfully and loyally.

God demanded that His children love Him and love their neighbor. Both of these great commandments are repeatedly referred to in the sacred Jewish literature.

Man was to be obedient and faithful to God by complete dedication to Him. Jews were to love and be concerned for others, especially their fellow Jews, but also for people of other nations and races.

Naturally, men did not always act in this fashion; they were sinners. Yet if they repented and asked God's forgiveness, He would always show mercy to them and would accept them again as His faithful people. Someday, perhaps when God's kingly rule was established, all men would be faithful to the Law and its commands. Every Jew looked toward this time with eager expectation.

In an earlier day, Jewish belief in a life after death was rather vague and unformed. Those who died did not altogether pass out of existence; they went to Sheol, a kind of underworld where they eked out a shadowy, inactive existence. But by the time of the Maccabees, many Jews began to change their belief about life after death. The Pharisees strongly supported the idea of the "resurrection of the dead," but the Sadducees rejected this belief. The teaching about the resurrection emphasized that the dead would be restored to life, both physically and in spirit when God would establish His kingdom. But by the time of Jesus, some Pharisees probably regarded the dead as already raised and united with God.

The strange figure known as John the Baptist should be considered against this background. Actually, he should be called John the Baptizer, since he demanded that those who heard and accepted his message should be baptized or undergo a "washing" in the river Jordan. John was an ascetic, world-denying preacher who went about the countryside proclaiming that the Jewish people must return to their devotion to the God who had chosen them in ages long past. So disloyal had they been to God and His will that a complete change in attitude was demanded of them. God was soon to show Himself, John proclaimed, and He would judge the nation with fire. Only those who repented would be able to withstand that judgment. Just as a non-Jew had to undergo baptism to become one of the chosen people, so all Jews should undergo baptism in the same way. For they had all been disloyal to God and had put themselves, in spirit and in attitude, apart from the people of God, however much they might still be Jews in name.

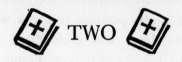 TWO

THE EARLIEST TRADITIONS ABOUT JESUS

It is actually impossible to write a biography of Jesus.

This statement may seem incredible but all modern New Testament scholars would surely agree. It does not mean that nothing can be said about his life, or that the broad outlines of his life are completely obscure. But it does mean that a straight biography of Jesus would be more the product of the author's imagination than the result of an informed and scientific use of available documents.

It is possible, however, to speak with considerable assurance about what Jesus said and taught and did. No one doubts that genuine historical events are described in the four gospels, and that the impact of

Jesus on his contemporaries is recorded in the New Testament. It is also possible to speak with assurance about the way Jesus was understood by the early Christian church. The entire New Testament is witness to that understanding. It reflects the significance that the first Christians and their immediate successors, up to the early years of the second century, found in Jesus. It tells us about his place in their own experience as his disciples, or followers, and also about how this experience produced their convictions about God, the world, and human history. All this is important in understanding the kind of person Jesus must have been and what he did during his lifetime.

No responsible scholar today accepts what is called the "Christ-myth theory" about the origins of Christianity. Originating in the nineteenth century, the theory views the story of Jesus and the figure of Jesus himself as the creations of the early Christians. He was said to be a mythological being put together out of the dreams, hopes, and fancies of men whose major concern was to establish a religious faith that would satisfy what people feel to be their deepest needs. The materials for this mythology were drawn from Jewish ideas prevalent at the time; from the "mystery religions," in which a god was believed to have entered the world to redeem men from slavery; and from other movements in the Near East.

Two experts in New Testament studies—F. C.

Conybeare, a non-believer, and Alfred Loisy, an ex-communicated Roman Catholic priest—have shown that the evidence proves the Christ-myth theory cannot be defended. While many ways of interpreting Jesus come from a variety of sources, the fact is, as these scholars pointed out, that sombeody had to exist in the first place to have his ideas interpreted at all. No responsible historian could deny this. Loisy, who was skeptical in his approach to matters of history, insisted that Jesus was a historical person about whom considerable information was to be known. He also showed that there was much interpretation even in the gospels, about which he was an acknowledged expert. But at the same time he demonstrated that the humble Jewish teacher was by no means a creation of fancy. He was a man who had lived and taught, had been arrested, and later crucified. Loisy had no doubt whatever that it was this historical person, and not a mythological figure, whom the earliest Christians believed—rightly or wrongly—had been "raised from the dead" and whom they therefore regarded as their divine Lord.

What kind of material exists that gives men the right to say anything at all about Jesus? The answer is that we possess the "earliest traditions" about him. We must discover their nature, their development, and the way in which they have been handed down in what are called the gospels, the first four books of the New Testament.

Careful and detailed study of gospel material has been going on for over a century. This kind of study is called gospel criticism. The word "criticism" here means that the methods of scholarship used in the study of ancient documents are used to study the first four books of the New Testament. No Christian believer should be alarmed at bringing such methods to bear on a subject that he regards as sacred. If Christianity is historical religion, whose central figure is believed to be a historical person, then the usual methods of historical study are necessary. The nineteenth-century English scholar Benjamin Jowett of Oxford once said that the Bible must be studied like any other book; only then will it be possible to say that it is not like any other book.

The first step in a critical study of the gospels is to establish the accuracy of the texts. This textual criticism has been carried on for a long time. The accepted results show that, in general, the material that is translated in the Revised Standard Version, for example, represents the actual text put down by the several authors, including minor errors of scribes. The discovery of several very ancient manuscripts, dating back to the first three or four centuries, gives a double assurance of the text. It is accepted that the gospels, with relatively slight alterations, are the words that the authors intended to write.

The second step in gospel criticism concerns the dating and arrangement of the material. There is some disagreement here among the experts, but, in general, most scholars claim that Mark's Gospel is the earliest of the four, dating about A.D. 65. The date for Matthew is usually given as A.D. 70 to 85, and for Luke, A.D. 80 to 90. John's Gospel is commonly regarded as having been last, and is dated between A.D. 95 and 105.

The first three gospels show a strong resemblance to each other. Stories and sayings are repeated almost verbatim in the original Greek. Many parallels, together with many differences, can be found in the treatment of the same event. There are obvious alterations of the material from one gospel to the other. The long-held theory is that the first gospel, Mark, was used by Matthew and Luke as a kind of framework for their own writings, but they both also had other material at hand that they used as well. That material is largely a collection of the sayings of Jesus.

For many Christians, John's Gospel has been the most loved of the four, because it concerns itself not so much with the narrative of events and the remembered teaching of Jesus, as with his significance. The first chapter tells how Christians thought of Jesus: he was "the Word made flesh"—God's outgoing movement to His world expressed uniquely in a man. The rest of the book is a series of portraits of Jesus as "the life of the world," "the light of men," and "the truth that makes men free." All of this is summed up in the seventeenth chapter where Jesus is portrayed as the supreme instance of God's love in action in the life of a man. In picturing Jesus in this way, the writer undoubtedly made use of traditions that had persisted in the Christian community, some of them from very early times. But his intention was not so much to give a picture of Jesus as he appeared in the days when he walked in Palestine, as it was to make clear what Jesus really meant to those who believed in him. One New Testament scholar has expressed this very well by applying phrases from the New Testament to the four gospels. The first three gospels tell "what the eye saw and the ear heard," as remembered in the early church; the fourth gospel tells "what it entered into the heart of man to conceive" about who Jesus was and what he meant to those who became his followers.

Who wrote the four gospels? Perhaps that question can never be answered. Certainly the gospel attributed to Luke and the book known as the Acts of the Apostles give the history of Christian origins. There is good reason to think that Luke himself, a companion of the apostle Paul, was the author of his gospel. As for the gospels of Matthew and Mark, nobody is certain who the writers were, although early Christian tradition ascribes the first gospel to one of the disciples and the second to a young man who was another of Paul's companions. The authorship of the fourth gospel has been the subject of much study and discussion, but no conclusions have been reached. Most think that the writer was not the "disciple whom Jesus loved" (whose name was said to be John), but perhaps a second-generation Christian who had known John, had been much influenced by him, and had used some of John's recollections of Jesus in compiling the gospel.

A third kind of New Testament critical study that has become more and more important in recent years is known as form criticism. This is the investigation of the forms, or small sections, composing the gospels. Each gospel is made up of stories, narratives, and accounts, all more or less self-contained units and fairly easy to separate from one another. Each form is composed of a few verses, as in the present versions of the Bible, sometimes two or three verses, sometimes ten or more. This form research has been carried on for many years, both in the study of the Old Testament and of many other ancient collections of events and sayings. The great experts in form criticism were the Germans Martin Dibelius, Rudolf Bultmann and K. L. Schmidt, and this type of study continues to be carried on by scholars of many countries.

The form critics not only attempt to classify the various sections, they also attempt to discover the actual situation in which these sections were first shaped. Since all the gospels had their origin in the recollections of the early Christian believers, the experts insist that the material was arranged to meet the needs of the Church in its preaching and teaching about Jesus. Each section intended to speak directly to people who were either already full members of the Church or were under instruction for membership. Therefore, each section had a place in the life of the Christian fellowship and in the faith of early Christian believers. Sometimes they are directly related to the worship of the Christian fellowship. The stories, including both what Jesus did and said, must have been shaped to some degree by the Christian community in its earliest years.

If this were true, it might be difficult to consider the gospels as a record of genuine history. However, the point to remember is that the way in which the gospels tell what happened is not the way of a cold, objective writer of a chronicle or a biography. Rather it is that of a believing and worshiping group of Christians, who told stories about a real man, Jesus, because they were his followers and wished others also to follow him. Yet, the form critics have made a great contribution to understanding the New Testament more fully. It is now possible to see how the different parts were shaped into a particular structure, and even, to some extent, colored in content by the deep faith of those first believers. Therefore, it is impossible to read the gospels as if they were simply four biographies of one man. The reader must identify with the thought, belief, and worship of the first Christians. He must look at what the gospels have to tell and understand it in the terms that those writers used.

The various forms in the New Testament have been roughly arranged into four categories: pronouncements; tales of Jesus' "mighty works," or miracles; legends or stories about Christ; and passion narratives.

The pronouncements consist of "sayings" that are attributed to Jesus—his teachings. Each contains a setting in which the teaching is said to have taken place; a reference to an action, however brief, of Jesus'; and the saying itself.

Here is the brief pronouncement section from Mark 2:18–22 that gives us Jesus' comments on the Jewish practice of fasting:

Now John's disciples and the Pharisees were fasting; and people came and said to him, "Why do John's disciples and the disciples of the Pharisees fast, but your disciples do not fast?" And Jesus said to them, "Can the wedding guests fast while the bridegroom is with them? As long as they have the bridegroom with them, they cannot fast. The days will come, when the bridegroom is taken away from them, and then they will fast in that day. No one sews a piece of unshrunk cloth on an old garment; if he does, the patch tears away from it, the new from the old, and a worse tear is made. And no one puts new wine into old wineskins; if he does, the wine will burst the skins, and the wine is lost, and so are the skins. But new wine is for fresh skins."

In each of the pronouncement sections, it is clear that the main concern is with Jesus' teaching.

The tales about Jesus' "mighty works" usually include the placing of the event, some action of Jesus' (usually the healing of a person), and the results that followed. These may be a visible result of the healing or a comment made about what has happened.

The following tale is from Mark 4:37–41:

On that day, when evening had come, he said to them, "Let us go across to the other side." And leaving the crowd, they took him with them, just as he was, in the boat. And other boats were with him. And a great storm of wind arose, and the waves beat into the boat, so that the boat was already filling. But he was in the stern, asleep on the cushion; and they woke him and said to him, "Teacher, do you not care if we perish?" And he awoke and rebuked the wind, and said to the sea, "Peace! Be still!" And the wind ceased, and there was a great calm. He said to them, "Why are you afraid? Have you no faith?" And they were filled with awe, and said to one another, "Who then is this, that even the wind and sea obey him?"

The legends or "stories about Christ" concern actions of Jesus' that do not involve miracles or mighty works. The stories are usually told to explain a belief or practice in the early days of the Christian church.

One legend is the brief account of Jesus' baptism, from Mark 1:9–11:

In those days Jesus came from Nazareth of Galilee and was baptized by John in the Jordan. And when he came up out of the water, immediately he saw the heavens opened and the Spirit descending upon him like a dove; and a voice came from heaven, "Thou art my beloved Son; with whom I am well pleased."

The passion narratives are somewhat different from the other three. They are longer and more closely knit. Very likely they have been enlarged by additional material, but they seem to be a continuous narrative based on remembered events, even though these events have been colored by the faith of the first Christian church. The passion narratives are very long and can be read in the first three gospels. They include the account of Jesus' entrance into Jerusalem on Palm Sunday and the events preceding his crucifixion and death. These accounts are simple and moving in their simplicity. It is possible to trace the way in which, over and over again, reference is made to Old Testament texts.

The first two chapters of Matthew and Luke also contain the stories of Jesus' conception and birth. These sections are generally considered separate from the rest of the material in the first three gospels. The sections that tell of Jesus' birth and of the occurrences that preceded it were probably written and arranged for a particular purpose by the writers of the Matthew and Luke gospels. They are attempts to indicate the significance that early Christians found in the life and mission of Jesus. The writers show this by saying that his unusual impact on those who knew him was due to the unusual circumstances of his birth. These circumstances are the direct action of God in bringing Jesus into the world. This material is "legendary" in character, meaning that it is a highly poetical story told about a great person for the purpose of establishing his significance. For this reason, the nativity narratives are not used when giving an account of what Jesus actually is remembered to have said and done. The story of Jesus in a historical sense must begin with his baptism by John the Baptizer, and not with the tales told about his birth and childhood.

As has been said, John's Gospel is in a different category from the other three. The material in it relies, almost certainly, on remembered traditions, but the writer does not handle it in the same way that the other writers handle their material. He does not string the sections together, but works out a pattern. Then he produces a sort of composite portrait to get his points across. The best way to study the fourth gospel is to read it as a whole, in order to understand the main emphasis in the portrayal of the dominant figure.

Someone has said that the gospels are like a series of impressionistic paintings of a remarkable man. They are sketches that show how Jesus was "received"— understood, appreciated, accepted, or rejected—by those who knew him. They are based on the oral tradition passed on by the very first Christians, who told what they had learned about Jesus from those who instructed them for membership in the Church. The gospels concern someone who really lived, at a particular time and in a particular place. They cannot be rejected as unhistorical because they were written from material handed on "from faith to faith." As they stand, they are witness to the truly overwhelming impact that Jesus made upon men and women.

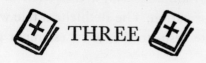

THREE

THE THINGS
JESUS DID

The best way to understand the things Jesus did is first to study the gospels, beginning with Mark, then Luke, and finally Matthew. Then it is possible to understand more fully the following broad sketch of his words and deeds.

Jesus was probably born in Nazareth, in the northern part of Palestine called Galilee, about 6 or 7 B.C. Although the Christian era begins from his birth, historical research has shown that he was actually born several years before the date that we acknowledge. The story that puts his birth in Bethlehem is regarded by most New Testament scholars as unhistorical. Of course, it was not intended to be a "lie" by those who related the story. Rather, it was one of the early tales in the Christian *haggadah,* a collection of stories and general information. The Bethlehem tale was probably told to relate Jesus to the Old Testament prophecy of his coming.

Nazareth was, and still is, a small town in the north country. It is not far from the Lake of Galilee, and is near the highway that was the main travel and trade route from the north down to Jerusalem and places south on the way to Egypt. Nazareth was in the domain of Herod Antipas, ruler of Palestine. The town seems to have been a center for the surrounding countryside of farmers and shepherds.

Jesus was the son of Mary, a young girl who, according to tradition, was both pious and faithful in her religious outlook, and of Joseph, an older man whose occupation was probably equivalent to that of a village handyman. "Carpenter" is not quite the right translation for the word in the gospels used to describe his work. It is better translated as "artisan"—which is to say that Joseph was a skilled mechanic. There seem to have been other, later children of this marriage. But we know little about them except for the few references to Jesus' brothers and sisters scattered here and there in the records. It seems that Joseph died while Jesus was a boy, and that Jesus probably carried on his father's occupation.

The home was devout and the life of the family typically Jewish, with affection among the members under the leadership of the father, who, like all Jewish fathers, was the master of the household. Joseph must have been a good and loving father, and the intimacy and affection that Jesus later manifested in his relationship with God must have been influenced by the affection he had known from Joseph. What little is told about his mother indicates that she was a loving parent, even though she is said to have found it difficult to understand what her elder son later took to be his vocation in life.

Jesus, along with his family, probably took part in regular worship at the local synagogue. He would have attended the village school that was held in the synagogue, and become familiar with the Jewish scriptures and their interpretations. His later teachings indicate very clearly that he knew the sacred writings of his people almost "by heart." He was equally informed about the way in which rabbis had tried to relate the sacred writings of the Torah to the current life of the Jewish people.

It is sometimes said that Jesus was a Galilean peasant. This is hardly accurate. His family was probably of the lower middle class of the time, but they were not peasants in the sense of people who worked the land. Unquestionably, however, he and his family belonged to "the people of the land," in the sense that they were hard-working, with neither time nor opportunity to obey every precise detail of the Law. Attend-

ance at synagogue worship, education at the village
school, and genuine piety in respect to Jewish belief
did not necessarily mean strict following of Jewish
practice. One of the charges made against Jesus in later
years was that while he knew the writings of the Torah,
he did not observe all the details they were thought
to require. Even if he was called rabbi, or teacher and
interpreter of the ancient Jewish Law, he did not have
the usual, formal rabbinical training, and he was not
so meticulous in his handling of the Law as rabbis
usually were.

John the Baptist, with his insistent summons to the
Jewish people to "repent" and to "save yourselves from
the wrath which is coming upon you," evidently made
a great impression on Jesus. By the time John began
to preach, Jesus was about thirty years old. Jesus had
spent his entire life up until this time, so far as is
known, making his home in Nazareth with his mother
and family. Perhaps he had gone on occasional trips
elsewhere; possibly he had visited the great city of
Jerusalem. And then came the mission of John. John's
message was delivered to crowds of men and women
who came from all over the land to see and hear this
hermitlike man. He dressed in a robe of camel's hair
and ate only the food that could be found in the wild
desert country.

What John had to say to the people was not very
comforting. He told them that the "end" was near—the

46

time when God would come in anger to purge the Holy
Land. That message was not new. What *was* new was
John's declaration that to be saved from destruction
they could not even rely on the fact that they were
Jews. They must "repent." They must return to the
way that God had laid down for them; they must
"bring forth fruits worthy" of the new start. Those who
heard his preaching perhaps did not remain with him
long, although there is some evidence that a company
of baptists, or followers, was formed and continued in
existence for a few decades. Those who heard him and
accepted the truth of what he said underwent a baptism
in the Jordan River—a ceremony that was the way of
starting them on a new life, now they had been restored
to God's favor and were determined to do His will.

Jesus, too, went to hear John preach. And having
heard his message, Jesus was baptized by John. It was
through that baptism that Jesus became aware of his
own mission in life. The gospels say that Jesus' baptism in the river Jordan brought about a profound inner change in Jesus, who believed he had received a
summons to act in a special way. He immediately
went into the nearby desert country to think through
this summons and to determine how it was to be carried out. Whether or not all this happened, the gospels
make it clear that Jesus was then faced with a momen-
tous decision about his life and work. Jesus soon became certain that his mission should be one of teaching

and preaching, of helping and serving. He was to continue John's kind of mission, but with a difference. Everything that was now to follow in the life of Jesus, up to and including his arrest and death, was to be the result of his faithful dedication to the mission he assumed.

After his baptism did Jesus begin to think of himself as the coming "Messiah"? Did he believe that he was the divinely empowered figure that many Jews expected would inaugurate the coming "kingdom of God"? The gospels seem to say that he did so regard himself, but that he wished to keep his conviction a secret. However, it appears more likely that Jesus did not think of himself as the Messiah. Jesus must have felt his mission to be prophetic, for like the great ancient Jewish spokesmen for God, he was to move about the country announcing the coming of the kingdom. This is, in a sense, what John the Baptizer had done. Jesus was to "go about doing good," boldly calling men to repentance. He would do this as one who had been called, who had been chosen by God precisely for this purpose. He was to be "a man under authority" from God, whom he called "Father." God had chosen him for this work and would give him the strength to fulfil his mission.

But Jesus did not begin his work immediately. His mission was to begin only after John was imprisoned by Herod whose matrimonial adventures the preacher had denounced.

After John was delivered up, Jesus came into Galilee preaching the good news of God: "the time is ripe and God's reign is near; repent, and believe this good news."

These are the words in Mark's Gospel that tell of the beginning of Jesus' own ministry. The proclamation is the same as that made by John himself.

Jesus began his mission by gathering about him men who probably were already well known to him. Peter and his brother Andrew; James and John, the sons of Zebedee; and others were "called" to be with him and to share in his proclamation of the coming reign of God. The "calling" may have been a matter of days or it may have been soon after John was imprisoned. In any event, Jesus had with him a group of close associates, with Peter as their leader, and they accompanied him from town to town and finally to Jerusalem.

The story of his preaching in the synagogue at Capernaum shows two outstanding features of his work. First of all, Jesus taught with authority. The witness of the gospels suggests that at Capernaum and elsewhere Jesus did not follow the usual rabbinical method of referring everything to the authority of the Torah. He spoke in a fresh, striking, and clear way of what

49

God demanded of his people. Like the ancient prophets, he went directly to the heart of the matter without referring to the great collection of learned discussion. This is what is meant by saying that Jesus had a
quality of authority. Today we would say that he was
a vivid and masterful person, sure of his message and
sure of himself in proclaiming it. John had proclaimed that the kingdom was coming. Jesus did the
same, but when he spoke the people felt that here was
no secondhand message. This one came straight from
God.

Jesus also had remarkable power to heal those who
were ill. His magnetic influence brought astounding results. For example, an overexcited, probably de-
ranged man once shouted out while Jesus was speaking. In telling him to be silent, Jesus quieted him and
restored him to his senses. Or again, a story in Mark's
Gospel tells that the mother-in-law of Simon Peter was
ill. Jesus healed her so that she was able to resume her
household duties.

However, the gospels are insistent that Jesus did not
want to be known primarily as a healer of the sick; he
was not a miracle worker. Yet when confronted by a
sick person he was able to speak words that brought
about either a cure or a real improvement in the person's condition. This power gave Jesus a fame that
was embarrassing to him—so much so that he tried to
get away from the crowds who came to him for cures.

He did not want to reject them, yet he did not want his real mission to be misunderstood.

Even allowing for the probability that these stories of healing have been exaggerated, there still remains a solid body of material in which this ability of Jesus is plainly remembered and stated. Of course, the medical diagnosis is always uncertain. Modern physicians would surely not describe sickness in the way the earliest Christians understood it. Jesus himself ascribes the healing to the faith of the people who were helped, rather than to any special skill of his own. It may be that his masterful personality, his forthright and vigorous way of speaking and acting, and his own strong faith in God evoked from sick people all their hidden recuperative powers. Those who were mentally disturbed may have been helped by Jesus' strong personal conviction, his authoritative manner, his deep concern, and his calm assurance of God's presence.

The impression of strength, along with Jesus' own faith in God and his conviction that he was speaking and acting on God's behalf, is also behind other stories that tell of his nature miracles. An example is the stilling of a storm on the Lake of Galilee, which threatened to drown him and those with him in the boat. The point of the story is that Jesus' personal confidence and faith during the storm awakened a similar confidence and faith in his disciples. Later, as the story was handed down, the "calming" referred to the storm itself. This transfer did not seem unnatural to Christian believers. If Jesus spoke and acted for God, why should he not have God's power over the forces of nature? The intention of the story is plainly stated in the last words of the account: "Who is this, that even the wind and the sea obey him?" The answer, as the primitive Christian church firmly believed, was that this was God's supreme representative, the Messiah himself. So overwhelming was the sense of Jesus' authority, so vivid was his personal mastery, that stories of such mighty works would almost inevitably be told. It is not necessary to accept as historically true every detail of any given gospel story. It is only essential to realize that such tales give witness to the authority of Jesus' figure.

There is no way to trace the precise sequence of events in Jesus' life after the baptism, the call of the first disciples, and the beginning of the preaching mission with its healings. However, for several months, perhaps a year, Jesus and his companions went about the Palestine countryside proclaiming the message of God's kingdom.

What Jesus taught about God, he embodied in his own life. He went out to "seek and save" those who were lost. He cared deeply for the people to whom he talked. He helped them in their sickness, both mental and physical, although he did not want to be known primarily as a "healer." He was happy in the company of the poor and simple, and friendly with women and children. The impression from the gospels is that Jesus was the personal embodiment of what we might call "loving concern." When he spoke sternly it was because he was outraged by the meanness, arrogance, pride, cruelty, and hatred he saw in men.

Opposition to Jesus and his mission developed quickly from those who interpreted the Law in the old way. As Jesus cut through the interpretative material, what he saw as the truth frequently turned out to be contrary to accepted ideas. For instance, when he said that "nothing that goes into a man, but what comes out of him, is what makes him unclean" (Mark 7:15), he was contradicting the notion about observance of the Jewish Law. Yet when he said that the care of one's parents has priority over the fulfillment of a religious vow, he was speaking in agreement with the Talmud or the accumulated body of interpretation. This saying, in Mark 7:9–13, indicates once again that much of what Jesus said was not new, yet the authority with which he said it seemed very new indeed.

Jesus soon became unpopular with many of the Jewish leaders. He was not excommunicated or persecuted, but simply derided. As a result, he stopped preaching and teaching in the synagogues. He discovered that the best place to speak was "in the open" and wherever he could find those who would listen to what he had to say. It is said that "the common people heard him gladly." They were attracted by the directness and authority of his manner and were drawn to him personally. However, Jesus did not want popularity. He wanted a genuine response from those who would take his message with seriousness and would repent, so that they might enter God's kingdom when it came.

He wanted his hearers to live as befits the children of God. He believed that only in that way would they be ready to receive the kingdom. The kingdom was for the generous, the neighborly, the loving, the loyal and true. That was the test that would be applied when God established in the world His sovereign control over the affairs of men. The very popularity of Jesus, coupled with the willingness of his followers to pay homage to him as the preacher, was indeed a trouble to him. "Why do you call me 'Master' yet not practice what I tell you is God's will?" he asked.

Jesus did not preach his message alone. He sent his disciples out on their own missions, to speak the same message and to speak it "in his name"—with his authority, by his direction, and in his spirit. The disciples met with considerable success. Yet Jesus was not interested mainly in the kind of response that they found. The significant thing was that they, like him, were doing God's work.

Sometime during this first part of Jesus' ministry, John the Baptizer sent messengers to inquire about Jesus and his work. John seems to have been given the impression that Jesus was perhaps less severe in his demands than John himself had been. Jesus drank wine; he enjoyed eating with others; he lacked the terrible sternness of John. Perhaps this was because Jesus had substituted love for John's righteousness as the central attribute of God and the real meaning of God's demands on his people. The difference between the two is the kind of character that God is said to have and the attitude of God to His human children. In John's preaching, God would come to punish men. In Jesus' preaching, God loved men and yearned for them to return to Him in faith, obedience, and love. There is a sternness in Jesus' preaching about God, to be sure, but that sternness is the quality that true love must always show in the presence of everything that needs change. For Jesus, God is like the best of Jewish fathers, but He is much more than that. The best of Jewish fathers was the master of his family and he was loving to all the members. For Jesus, God is Lord of the whole world and loves every human being in it. For Jesus, God wishes to win men by His love rather than drive them by His power. Not that Jesus thought of God in a sentimental, easygoing fashion. But for him the heart of his message was that God was coming to express Himself in love, and "the wrath of God"—His sternness and righteousness—was to be seen only in His rejection of all that was loveless and mean. God's wrath was the unyielding and unbending quality of His love in action. God wished His people to revere Him, but He did not want them to be scared of Him. The way they would show their reverence was by loving others as God Himself loved all men.

Very likely, the opposition to Jesus soon led him to see that he was not going to be successful in any obvious way. Perhaps, too, the period during which he went off for a brief rest gave him time to evaluate how effective his preaching mission was in bringing about the changes he desired. Certainly the fact that Jewish leaders refused to listen to him must have had an effect upon his own view of his work. Jesus now decided to change the course of his mission. He knew that if he went to Jerusalem and denounced the nation and its leaders for their disregard of the will of God, he would risk arrest and even death. Yet he decided that this must be his course. The gospels say he predicted the eventual result in very explicit terms, but most scholars think that this is not so. Yet his attitude, and the bold way in which he seems to have faced his opposition, do make it seem that he was under no illusions whatever about the final result.

Two incidents have great importance in this connection. One is the so-called confession of faith by Peter at Caesarea Philippi, a Roman town northeast of Galilee; the other is the vision of Jesus that Peter and others experienced in the incident known as the Transfiguration. The historical basis for these accounts in the gospel is not entirely clear, yet they must have had some grounding in the actual course of his mission.

The confession of faith came after Jesus asked his disciples to tell him who they thought he represented. After some hesitation, Peter said that Jesus was the Messiah, the agent of God who was to bring in the divine kingdom. Jesus answered that if this were so, then the work of the Messiah would have to be accomplished through death. This indicates that whatever Jesus thought about himself, and however his disciples regarded him, he was clearly aware of the tragic aspect of his mission. "The Son of Man must be put to death. . . ." Both the pressure of events and Jesus' own deepest thoughts about what he was doing had brought him to the conviction that only through his death would he be able to fulfill God's purpose.

The second incident concerning Jesus and the death he foresaw relates how a few of Jesus' disciples saw him "glorified" by God, who had chosen him as His "beloved son." It includes the report that Moses and Elijah were with Jesus in his glorification. In Jewish thinking, these two men stood for the whole teaching of the Old Testament. Their appearance with Jesus was taken to indicate that what he was doing—as well as what he was himself—confirmed Jewish faith and hope in God's purpose for His people. The Law and the prophets—the whole past history of the Jewish people in their relationship with God—were shown to have reached their culmination in Jesus and his mission.

The story of the Transfiguration is variously interpreted today. Some scholars say that it really happened after Jesus' resurrection. Others think that it refers to some vision or perhaps even a dream that the disciples experienced during their days with Jesus in Palestine. Whatever the case, the incident is testimony to the conviction that instead of contradicting all that Judaism stood for, Jesus was the fulfillment and completion of Jewish expectation. It is through the evil in the world and the death that every man must face that God's will is accomplished. Jesus accepted this interpretation. He did so with complete serenity, certain that God is sovereign over His world, no matter how terrible may be the experiences that men must endure.

As Jesus understood his mission, he would have to go up to Jerusalem, the religious and civil capital of the country. He must challenge the leaders of his people with his message. The result would doubtless be his arrest and death. If so, that was part of the divine purpose for him. If this were "the cup" that Jesus must drink, he would drink if fully. It was a matter of "not my will, but thine be done."

That prayer, which the gospels report was offered in the Garden of Gethsemane just before Jesus' arrest, does not mean that Jesus passively accepted a terrible, unavoidable fate. On the contrary, Jesus in effect was saying "Not my own human idea of what might be good and desirable but the profound purpose of God, this must be accomplished. And since it must be accomplished through me, I accept it fully, completely, gladly. Thy will, O God, be done—and let it be done through my own willingness to be used in its fulfillment." This emphasis explains why the stories in the gospels do not picture Jesus as a reluctant martyr going to his end. Rather they portray a masterful, majestic, even victorious figure on his way to the accomplishment of his chief purpose in life.

Jesus went up to Jerusalem. Along the way a number of incidents occurred. For example, he took a child in his arms, saying that the kingdom is to be received in a fashion that is genuinely childlike. This story probably reflects in part the love of Jesus for children, but it was also intended to show that the only way in which anyone can live before God is with acceptance of the Father's will and the simplicity of faith that a child has for his human father and in the father's love for him.

Another incident concerns the young man—the "rich young ruler"—who came to ask Jesus what he must do to enter God's kingdom. Jesus answered that he should follow the commandments of the Jewish Law. But the young man had already done that; still he felt that something was lacking. Perhaps he wished to be accepted as one of Jesus' followers. In that case, he would have to leave behind all his possessions and live a simple life. The young man was not prepared for that kind of renunciation, and so he turned away. The disciples wondered about this and asked Jesus who indeed could enter the kingdom. And Jesus answered that with God anyone can enter the kingdom, so they must not judge by human standards. The final test would always be the degree of sacrifice that a man was prepared to make to achieve the highest goal.

James and John, the sons of Zebedee, wanted assurance that when God's kingdom did come, they would be part of it—"on either hand of Jesus in his glory," for it was assumed that Jesus would be lord of the kingdom when it came. Instead, they were rebuked by Jesus for desiring personal dominion. His disciples were to be servants of men, not those who strive for lordship over men. And he said: "Even as the Son of Man did not come to be ministered unto, but to minister, and to give his life a ransom for many." A man's place in God's kingdom would be determined by his willingness to serve others. So every follower of Jesus was to be what Jesus himself was, "a man for others."

What of those words concerning the Son of Man, where Jesus himself seems to be the subject? What of the words about "giving his life as a ransom for many"? What can they mean? Perhaps most New Testament experts believe that they reflect the early Christian conviction that "God in Christ reconciled the world to Himself," and through Jesus' death established a new relationship between men and Himself. Jesus was the "ransom" for men from slavery to sin because he died to restore them to sonship with God. But the words may actually have come from Jesus himself, although if so, they must be understood in a different sense than in developed Christian belief. Perhaps they were intended to indicate that by accepting God's will to the point of dying, Jesus would fulfill his task of bringing men to God.

Jesus entered Jerusalem, the holy city of the Jews. His entrance, the gospels say, was accompanied by acclamation from the crowd of people who were on their way to observe the great Passover feast. Thousands of pilgrims came every year to be present at the feast. Doubtless the "prophet" of Nazareth, whose preaching had become a matter of general discussion throughout the land, was welcomed into the city. The people shouted traditional Jewish psalms and greeted Jesus as one who clearly spoke God's will and cared for his fellow Jews.

Then comes the account in the gospels of the cleansing of the Temple. This event becomes important because it seems to have been the overt incident that led to Jesus' arrest. He denounced the way in which the outer court of the holy place was being used to extort money from the worshipers. Jesus did not denounce the accepted Jewish practice of Temple sacrifice. He decried the commercial and professional way that worship was conducted. He attacked the practice of cheating simple people when they exchanged money to buy the animal sacrifice that was to be offered on their behalf. He criticized the lack of devoutness. Jesus wanted simplicity, earnestness, the intention to obey God's will, and a witness to that will for all mankind. If the Jewish people and their leaders really believed in the God who had chosen them, if they really understood that God loved and cared for them, they should see that God wanted them to express their faith in simplicity, earnestness, and obedience. This was the "true religion." The inevitable result of true religion would be love for others and the strong desire to serve them in every possible way.

Jesus' stay in Jerusalem before his arrest is filled with incidents that help us to understand how he believed God wanted him to act. His remarks about the destruction of the Temple show this. He does not seem to have been much impressed by the magnificence of that great place of worship. Indeed, he is reported to have said that the building might be destroyed. "If this Temple were destroyed," he added, "I would build it in three days." This remark was used against him to justify his arrest and condemnation—he was a revolutionary, it was said.

Some interpreters have thought that Jesus' words did

not mean that he was announcing the actual destruction of the Temple, but was referring to his own body, which would be destroyed and raised up again. Another interpretation seems more likely. F. C. Burkitt, a Cambridge New Testament scholar, said that Jesus was asserting that if the Temple were indeed to be destroyed, everything that was really necessary for the true worship of God could be arranged in a very brief time. Sacrifices and a holy place were necessary, but not in as elaborate an establishment as the Jewish Temple had come to be. Simplicity, earnestness, "purity of heart," witness to all mankind that God was God—these, said Burkitt, were what Jesus really desired.

Another significant incident involved the discussion that Jesus had about what was truly essential in the life that God desired from his people. Mark says that a lawyer—a rabbinical interpreter of the Torah—wanted to know what was basic in Jewish religion. Jesus answered that it was the faith in the one God whom men were to love and serve, and that the inevitable extension of that faith was the love for one's neighbor.

Other incidents concern the way Jesus rejected the Zealots' defiance of the Roman authority. He approved the payment of Caesar's tax, provided that people also "render to God the things that God demands." In another story, Jesus rejected loyalty to himself if it was based on the supposed grounds of his kinship to the great King David of earlier days. Jesus' reference here was probably to his conviction that the one who would bring in God's kingdom would not be of regal descent but would be the representative of God as Father. It would be a "spiritual" messiah who would be the instrument for God's love, not a royal agent who would reestablish the Jews by military action.

The Last Supper, the meal Jesus shared with his disciples, took place just before Jesus' arrest. This was a table meal held just before the Passover feast was to begin in Jerusalem. As such, it was not unlike the many meals that Jesus had shared with his friends. It included the old Jewish table ritual of the breaking and sharing of bread and the drinking from a common cup. Jesus did and said the things that the leader of a group of Jews would habitually do at such a meal. But the very earliest Christian church came to believe that something else had also taken place. In breaking the bread and sharing the cup with his disciples, Jesus must have indicated that they were participants in his life and in his death. So the Last Supper in "the upper room" was the origin of the chief act of Christian worship through all succeeding ages. It was both a celebration of the good things given by God and known to all Jews in their common life as well as the identification of the disciples with the willingness of Jesus to give his life "for many." ("For many" is equivalent to the Jewish idiom meaning "for all.") This identification is the sense of the words, "This my body," and "This my death [blood] to bring about a new covenant [relationship] between God and men."

The scene in the Garden of Gethsemane came just after the supper and before the arrest. There Jesus prayed to God his Father, in terrible earnestness and "with as it were drops of blood falling from his face," for strength to face the ordeal ahead of him. He prayed that if it were at all possible, he could wish to be spared this dreadful fate. Yet he was sure that God's will, and His love for him and for the world, included that destiny. So he asked that he be able to accept it with full faith and in complete readiness to do what was required of him. "Not my will, but thine *be done*."

Jesus was arrested shortly afterward by a band of soldiers sent from the Temple. He was given a preliminary hearing before the officials of the Temple, accused of plotting an insurrection, and was asked who he considered himself to be. In his answer he affirmed that he was in a most profound sense acting for God. He declared his conviction that God—and he, Jesus acting for God—would not be defeated but would triumph over suffering and death. Then he was sent to appear before the Roman governor, Pilate. The gospels suggest that Pilate was reluctant to impose the death penalty that was asked. Finally he was persuaded when he learned that Jesus was charged with planning an uprising against Roman rule. He sentenced Jesus to death. This was in the year A.D. 27.

And so Jesus was crucified. He carried the crossbeam on his back in the procession that made its way to the place appointed for his death. There the upright wooden beam was already in place. The Man of Nazareth was nailed to the crossbeam, and the beam was then lifted and firmly secured to the upright. And Jesus was left to die.

We read in the gospels of the "seven words from the Cross." But it is not known just how many or which of them were actually said by Jesus. Some have thought that all the words are from the early Christian interpretation of Jesus' death. They were chosen to stress its meaning and its fulfillment of Old Testament prophecy. Others have felt that "My God, my God, why hast thou forsaken me?"—the words Jesus cried out— must be authentic.

Even if Jesus had said nothing at all, it would still have been consistent with his willing acceptance of death as part of God's purpose. If he said "My God, my God, why hast thou forsaken me?" it would mean that at the last moment Jesus was in utter despair. His physical anguish was accompanied by an even greater mental anguish and an appalling sense of loneliness. But it is the Christian assurance that the Lord knows from His own experience the worst fate that can happen to any man: to feel that all he has stood for and believed in is meaningless; to feel that he has been deserted by the very God in whom he had put his trust. What is most important, not only for Christian belief but also for historical understanding, is the fact that Jesus did indeed die. Whatever may have been his feelings at the time of his death, he died because he had become absolutely convinced that this death was not meaningless. It was God's way of establishing His reign of justice in the world, and manifesting His self-giving love.

The gospels end with a series of stories about the Resurrection. Dr. Burkitt, in his book, *Christianity*, commented on the stories that tell of how the earliest followers of Jesus came to believe that he had conquered death:

It is unscientific to write a sketch, however short and one-sided, of the Life of Jesus and leave out the Resurrection. In a sense we know nothing of personages of past ages who have left no written or artistic memorials of their own: strictly speaking, we only know the impression they made. . . . In that sense the Resurrection of Jesus is a well-attested fact; the impression he made on Peter and those who shared Peter's experience was that he was alive again, that they saw him alive and that nothing could make them doubt it. The surviving traditions of these appearances of Jesus are confused and contradictory: there can be little doubt that there is an element of unhistorical legend and even fancy in some of the tales. . . . But they have one curious characteristic which they share with the experience of Saul on his way to Damascus and in which they differ from other gospel "miracles." The gospel wonder-tales, we are told, produced astonishment, but the effect was transitory: the "Feeding of the Five Thousand" did not make the disciples less anxious when they were short of provisions. . . . But neither Simon Peter nor Saul of Tarsus seem to have had any further doubts when once they had been persuaded that Jesus had appeared to them alive. . . . Jesus was speaking to them still, he was still alive. . . . It might be thought that such enthusiastic notions would gradually lose their vigour and fade. The odd thing is that they did not fade, but persisted.

 FOUR

THE THINGS
JESUS SAID

Jesus was not primarily a teacher. It is a mistake to regard him as one of the sages whose words of wisdom are always to be remembered—men such as Confucius or Socrates or even the "wise men" in Jewish history. What Jesus said was important to the earliest Christians because of what they believed he had done—his teaching helped them to understand who he was. It was also important because it was their clue to the criteria by which God would eventually judge His human children and determine whether or not they were worthy to enter His kingdom.

Jesus did not concern himself directly with the great moral issues and problems that have always confronted man. He did not analyze and discuss questions about ethics that philosophers have wrestled with throughout human history. Famous men, including Socrates and Confucius, Plato and Aristotle, and in more recent times, Immanuel Kant, were primarily interested in the meaning of concepts such as duty, responsibility, goodness, virtue, and happiness. They attempted to understand the significance of "free will" and "moral necessity." They were moral theorists. Jesus was not. What he said was always directed to particular issues in their immediate living context. He did not talk about what goodness means in an abstract sense; he was concerned with this or that good deed. He did not speak about love as a general notion. He illustrated the love that he believed marked God's character, and should also mark men's character, by telling a story about some loving action.

These two important points must be remembered when considering the things Jesus said: he did not claim to be a teacher of morals, and he was not a philosopher who discussed abstract questions. There is also a third, equally important point. Jesus was a Jew. The background of his thought, as well as the context of his teaching and the basis for it, was the Jewish conviction that God was the Lord of the universe and the ultimate determiner of human destiny. Jesus was not expounding some newly revealed truth for the first time. Somebody once said, "The originality of Jesus did not consist in his saying things that were entirely new; it consisted, rather, in his omissions—what he de-emphasized or entirely discarded in the long tradition of Jewish thought." However, some of the things Jesus said *were* new, at least from the point of view of his contemporaries.

The principles that emerge from the stories Jesus told or from his sayings are based upon his conviction, shared with all fellow Jews, that man's primary concern is to enact the will of God. Jesus did not say that men must continually be conscious of God in all they do. He did not judge men's behavior by whether or not they had the correct religious opinions. He said that many who do not consciously recognize God may be doing God's will.

The main points of what Jesus said must be gathered from his remembered teaching in the gospels. These are always in the context of the immediate situation with which Jesus was dealing. A large portion of what Jesus taught is also found in his parables.

A parable is sometimes confused with an allegory. An allegory is a story in which each character and every incident stand for some eternal truth or some highly important aspect or element in life, whether human or divine. A parable is a story that illustrates only one point. All the details contribute to that point. They make the story more lively, and give it a greater quality of truth. All the details in a parable are included to make the story a good story, one that people will listen to, that will help them understand their human situation, in which God would have them live and act in accordance with His purpose of justice and love.

Jesus' teaching is entirely based on God, His justice and love. Jesus did not say in so many words that God is love, but he told many stories and made many remarks that show clearly how basic this was to all his thinking. The kind of love that Jesus had in mind was not sentimental or soft. Even when he told such wonderful parables as the one about the loving father and the wasteful son—which should be called "The Loving Father" rather than "The Prodigal Son"—there is no sentimentality. "Love for Jesus is always an austere love," it has been said. The love of God for men is exacting and it makes demands upon them.

The other side of God's nature has to do with God as justice. Once again it would be a mistake to think that justice must always be unrelenting and impersonal. A father who simply indulges his children is only spoiling them by his failure to prepare them for a world where they will not always be able to get what they want. A father who is overbearing and too severe in dealing with his children will only make them embittered and very likely rebellious against him. It is by a combination of love and righteousness that a good father best trains his children. When he makes demands upon them, these demands are never arbitrary or entirely unrelated to their true nature. On the contrary, they are the way in which his love expresses itself for their best good. A good father must let his children see that it is his love that is basic to his justice and central in all his relationships with them. So it is with God as Jesus portrays Him. God is never arbitrary, never impersonal, never "mean" in dealing with men. He is utter and complete love; He wishes His human children to be utterly and completely loving, both toward Him and toward other people.

God is also profoundly concerned with each and every human being, and His concern is shown in a personal way. Critics have disagreed about whether Jesus taught that each man's own creation makes him "a son of God." Some say that this particular relationship is only for those who hear the news of God's kingdom and accept it with all their hearts. But no matter which interpretation is correct, Jesus did think of every human being as God's child, created by God, sustained and helped by God. Since everybody is God's child, Jesus said that God wanted everyone to act like His child—each man's life should reflect the character of his heavenly Father.

Jesus constantly used the word "father" when speaking of God, as well as to God. Of the few Aramaic words and phrases that are remembered from Jesus' teaching and found in the gospels, the word *abba*, "father," is used most frequently. If it is true that God is love, that justice is one of the ways in which

His love works, that He cares for each man personally as His child, then God may indeed be thought of as Father. This is not new with Jesus. The Jews, too, had called God "Father," although generally this meant for them, "Father of the chosen people," rather than Father of all men. What is unique in the teaching of Jesus is the intimacy and directness with which the fatherhood of God is portrayed and acted out in life.

The God who is the loving Father is also the God who has a purpose in the affairs of men and in the whole course of nature and history. He has cared for the world from the very beginning, and He will bring about the visible establishment of His reign in that world. However and whenever the kingdom comes, Jesus pictured God's reign as a state in which His purpose of love would be fully expressed. The exacting love of God would be accepted by His children and would be shown in every corner of men's lives. Men would not bring in the kingdom by being good and loving, or just and righteous. Those things would be the result of the coming of the kingdom. The kingdom itself would be brought about only by what God did.

What did Jesus say about his own place in the coming reign? This is a difficult, if not impossible, question to answer. Perhaps he identified himself with the Messiah; perhaps he thought of himself as "the Son of Man"; perhaps he felt that he was like the "suffering servant" mentioned in the Old Testament book of

Isaiah. The servant would experience pain and even death as the way in which God's love would be shown and His kingdom brought into the world. It may also be that Jesus thought that his function was to be the prophetic voice for God and the proclaimer of God's will and purpose. His future position would be exactly what God made it to be. If Jesus did think and perhaps say that about himself, then he was loyal to his vocation as he understood it. Actually Jesus did not talk much about himself; he talked about God.

Jesus believed that this world is God's world. He rejoiced in its beauty and delighted in finding disclosures of God in birds and flowers, in the changing of the seasons, in the ordinary affairs of men and women, in little children and their play. Jesus was in many ways what today would be called a "humanist," and he was criticized for his willingness to accept the world and the good things in it. This does not mean that he was unaware of evil, suffering, or wrongdoing. On the contrary, his teaching was full of examples in which bad things in men's lives were emphasized. He was not a foolish optimist who disregarded the uglier side of nature. But he was an optimist in his deep conviction that God was good, loving, just, and was able to handle the evil occurrences in the world.

As we have seen, Jesus insisted that men should respond to God's love by themselves expressing love toward one another. For him, that was the inevitable result of accepting the gospel. The love men should show in their lives originates in the fatherly love of God for each and every one. Its result is a life of service, where each uses whatever abilities he has for other people. Yet Jesus did not tell his hearers to love humanity in an abstract and general way. He told stories that pointed to an immediate and particular situation where service should be given.

The English writer G. K. Chesterton once remarked that Jesus did not teach us to love man but to love men. His teaching personalizes love. In the great picture of jugment in Matthew's Gospel, Jesus portrays the Son of Man as the divine ruler and judge of all men, who gives his final judgment based on human service. The only test is whether they have, in fact, fed the hungry, given drink to the thirsty, visited the sick, helped the prisoners, or clothed the naked. The Son of Man is represented as saying, "Inasmuch as ye have done it unto one of the least of these . . . ye have done it unto me." This is the point that is stressed in the parable of the Good Samaritan.

Jesus also said that inner attitudes determine the true character of a person. "The inside of the cup" must be made clean. The man who, deep in his heart, hates another person is himself a hateful person, even though he may put on an outward show of goodness.

Can people be ordered to love? Of course, Jesus did not discuss this question in the way a philosopher

might have done. But he indicated clearly that the
way in which love is generated is by loyalty to the love
that is God. What is commanded is the loving action—
actually, an order to love one's brother means an order
to do the loving thing for that brother. Positive, outgoing, self-giving concern for one's neighbor can be
developed, and this is what is ordered. What cannot
be ordered is the emotional attitude—liking another
person. But that attitude is not so important, in one
way, as the determination to cooperate fully with the
love that is God in action. Jesus was realistic about this.
He was also realistic in seeing that once a person really
begins to care for other people in this positive way,
his inner life is affected. Our habits of action begin to
color our "spiritual insides."

Jesus was equally sure, and taught in the plainest
way, that idle thoughts, momentary impulses, and
leisure hours all work to establish the sort of persons
we are going to be. Therefore, he said, we must use
every opportunity to do good; we must take the responsibility for doing good. We must also fix our
thoughts, so far as we are able, on that which is truly
good, namely on God Himself. Jesus simply told men
that they were to worship God, pray to Him trustingly
in an attitude of childlike obedience, and try to identify
their deepest desires with God's will for the world.
Then they would find themselves strengthened to love
their brothers.

Thus Jesus taught that what men are is more important than what they do. Yet what they do will be the expression of what they are. They will be judged by what they do, since that will prove whether they are the kind of people who can be admitted to God's kingdom. "By their fruits ye shall known them. Do men gather grapes from thorns, or figs from thistles?"

One writer commenting on Jesus' teaching has said that so far as men's actual day-by-day living is concerned, Jesus "calls people to an adventurous way of life." He wants them to live boldly and bravely. Yet he also told his hearers that they must "count the cost." This admonition is found in several parables. He wanted people to see that the adventurous view of life that love requires also demands that people be aware that it *is* risky and adventurous. To live lovingly is a dangerous enterprise. It exposes people to difficulties and misunderstandings. It raises many questions and demands hard decisions. It denies ease and self-satisfaction. Jesus himself knew this very well. He probably could have continued his life as an artisan in Nazareth. Certainly he did not have to go to Jerusalem to challenge the leaders of his people. Very likely he could have saved himself from death. All this might have happened if he had been willing to settle back in quiet and comfort. But having "counted the cost," he went forward in loving service as "the man for others," ready to take risks, with the certainty that the end of his mission would be his rejection and death.

We know that Jesus did not have a gloomy attitude toward death; neither did he have a gloomy attitude toward life. Much Christian devotion speaks of Jesus as a "Man of Sorrows." Jesus did sorrow over his failure to win his people to his message. Yet at the same time he was a man who enjoyed life. Jesus delighted in nature and also delighted in people. He may have been stern to those who were mean and unloving, but he was sympathetic to those who suffered and were in trouble. He was friendly with others and his whole attitude toward life could be called joyful.

The very first part of the Sermon on the Mount is referred to as "the Beatitudes." In most of the English versions of the New Testament, the word "blessed" is used to translate the Greek word *makarioi* found in these sayings. From that translation comes the term "beatitudes," or "blessednesses." But the Greek word in the Sermon really means happy. So we should read, *"Happy* are those who are poor in spirit . . . happy are those who mourn . . . happy are those who suffer for righteousness' sake . . . happy are the humble meek." Jesus was a happy man, and he wanted others to be happy too. And he told them how they could be most happy. That is what the Beatitudes are all about.

Happiness often suggests a superficial kind of gleefulness. This was not true for Jesus. His happiness was a deep and abiding joy that came when men and women were doing what was best for themselves and for others. He told people that they were to be "perfect, as the heavenly Father is perfect." Once again the Greek word is helpful. The word is *teleios,* and could be defined as "being fulfilled or being fully oneself." Or to put it more plainly: "Be yourselves, be full and true men who are God's children, just as God Himself is fully God—Himself utterly love and ceaselessly giving His love to His children." To be oneself brings real and inescapable happiness. It is joyful to realize to the fullest degree all of one's potentialities, to express them in outward actions, and to feel the deep satisfaction that comes from genuine integration of personality.

When Jesus used the idea of "satisfaction," he did not mean cheap pleasure or easy self-acceptance. Satisfaction meant being really oneself, making real all that it is possible to be. A writer has said that God's purpose for us is that we who are human shall become human and shall remain human. That is the point of Jesus' teaching here. Men are not to be animals, nor are they to try to be angels. They are not just physical bodies and they can never become disembodied spirits. They are men, beings both physical and spiritual, both "dust of the earth" and "living souls inbreathed by God." If that is what they are by the

80

fact of their creation, then that is how they are to act. When men act like that, they are deeply and truly satisfied. They are "perfect" in the only sense in which human beings can be perfect. It is then that they are really happy.

Jesus also said a good deal about what we call "the future life." He pictured this within the terms of the Jewish idea of "the resurrection of the body," rather than within the Greek idea of "the immortality of the soul." Jews did not think that there was a spirit that would be released from its bodily prison at the moment of death. Man was an organic whole, and any notion of "future life" must include both soul and body. This meant that God had created and sustained human beings as genuine personalities. When they died, all of them died. But the God who had created and sustained them could and would recreate them, so that they could share His life in His "heavenly kingdom."

Undoubtedly, Jesus accepted the popular beliefs about resurrection, but he never elaborated on them or described what a future life would be like. The present world is the place where men are engaged in shaping their personality. When John Keats spoke of the world as "a vale of soul-making," he was echoing what Jesus wished to communicate in his teaching. What we do here determines what sort of personalities we become. Dr. Bethune-Baker said that "in Jesus' teaching life is a trust committed to everyone born into the world.

Hereafter he will have to give an account of the trust. It is what he is making of it, stage by stage of his life, that makes him what he is; and what he is will determine his state in his future life, whether the Son of Man shall be ashamed of him (Mark 8:38 and parallels) or shall say to him, 'Well done, good and faithful servant' (Matthew 25:23)." Jesus urged men to live trustfully and responsibly, doing the good and righteous thing that opportunity offered or occasion demanded, believing that God who is love will take care of them in the way that is best. Thus, they need not be afraid to risk their lives for that which is good, righteous, and loving. The grain of the universe runs that way.

A great deal of what Jesus said is contained in the so-called Sermon on the Mount, which is really a collection of Jesus' teaching that the early Christians remembered. It is found in the fifth, sixth, and seventh chapters of Matthew, the first book of the New Testament, and has parallels in the sixth chapter of Luke's Gospel. This material, like all of Jesus' teaching, points to particular situations. It is full of paradoxes and aphorisms, while at the same time it makes what seem highly exaggerated assertions. The paradoxes are meant to provoke thought. For example, we are told that the way to real riches is by being poor. The aphorisms say that one should "give to everyone that asks you," "lend expecting nothing back," always "turn the other cheek," never "resist evil." It has been said that if the teaching in the Sermon on the Mount were faithfully followed, the structure of human society would topple down and men's lives would become utter chaos.

The confusion exists because people insist on taking what Jesus said in its most literal sense. They fail to recognize that he taught by allusion, by hyperbole, or exaggeration, and certainly very often with humor. Through the use of overstatement, and even ridiculous illustrations (in his teaching he spoke of a camel going through the eye of a needle), Jesus made his hearers think. He intended to do this, for he wanted people to make their own moral decisions. As a Jewish prophet, he sharpened his hearers' ideas of duty and truth in vivid and unforgettable language. Sometimes he said what seem quite contradictory things. The way to make sense of Jesus' teaching, especially when it is collected together as in the Sermon on the Mount, is to try to catch the spirit of his sayings and to be receptive to new possibilities. Read his words, not as if they were precise statements of moral laws, but as sharp, provocative clues to how we are to meet our problems in the spirit of loving concern.

Everything Jesus said expressed the conviction that God would shortly inaugurate His kingdom. But that kingdom did not come, certainly not in the way that Jesus must have expected it. What did come into being was a community of men and women who believed not only what Jesus said but believed in him. Alfred Loisy observed that Jesus preached and expected the coming of the kingdom of God, but it was the Christian church that appeared. Does this mean that Jesus was mistaken?

For all Christians there is a very profound belief that the "kingdom of God" was inaugurated in history when the fellowship of those who believed in Jesus was established. Those who took him as their "Lord and Master," who regarded him as God's agent and messenger, and who saw him as the means for God's own presence in the world were sure that he was still with them in their common worship and life. They were assured that in the life of love, obedience, and common sharing that marked the true Christian church there was a foretaste of that state when God will be truly visible in the total human enterprise. They may have been wrong about this, but that is what Christians thought to be the case. In that sense, Jesus was not mistaken at all, so far as the reality of the kingdom was concerned. He was mistaken only in the way in which, as a Jew, he described it.

Dr. A. N. Whitehead said:

The founders of Christianity and their earlier followers firmly believed that the end of the world was at hand. The result was that with passionate earnestness they gave free reign to their absolute ethical intuitions respecting ideal possibilities without a thought of the preservation of society. . . . A standard had now been created, expressed in concrete illustrations foolproof against perversions. This standard is a gauge by which to test the defects of human society. So long as the Galilean images are but the dreams of an unrealized world, so long they must spread the infection of an uneasy spirit.*

Whitehead is suggesting that because Jesus' teaching was "conditioned" by the expectation of "the end" and the coming of God's kingdom, it can remain a goal we must ceaselessly strive after and a goad that pricks our consciences, making us "uneasy" when we fail to live in terms of the absolute love and justice that God wants from His human children.

In the last analysis, what is the point of all that Jesus did and said? Dr. Whitehead sums it up this way:

The essence of Christianity is the appeal to the life of Christ as a revelation of the nature of God and of His agency in the world. The record is fragmentary, inconsistent, and uncertain. It is not necessary for me to express any opinion as to the proper reconstruction of the most likely tale of historical fact. . . . But there can be no doubt as to what elements in the record have evoked a response from all that is best in human nature. The Mother, the Child, and the bare manger: the lowly man, homeless and self-forgetful, with his message of peace, love, and sympathy: the suffering, the agony, the tender words as life ebbed, the final despair: and the whole with the authority of supreme victory.*

* *Adventures of Ideas*, London: Macmillan, 1933; New York: New American Library (Mentor Books).
* *Ibid.*

85

Whitehead is saying that in the things that Jesus did and in the things that Jesus said, we are assured that the divine agency in the world persuades but does not force. Together they demonstrate the truth about God and man, and about the true relationship existing between them. The truth about the kind of life that is proper to man is to be found in love—the kind of love shown in and by the man Jesus.

This is how Jesus in his life and in his sayings has made his enormous contribution to the world. Now we shall see the way in which the Christian community came to understand how he could be interpreted as the "revelation of the nature of God and of His agency in the world."

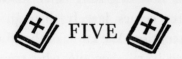 FIVE

HOW JESUS
WAS "RECEIVED"

Everything that we know about Jesus comes from
the traditions found in the Christian church in its
earliest days. These were handed down by word of
mouth within the fellowship of Christian believers.
There is no independent information about Jesus, except for some references to him and to Christians in
two or three outside sources. The Jewish historian
Josephus (A.D. 37–?100) mentions him; the Roman
historian Suetonius (A.D. ?69–?140) has a few words
about him. Another Roman historian, Tacitus (A.D.
?55–?117), refers to the people who followed Christ,
and the Roman government official Pliny (A.D.
23–79) speaks about Christians who "worship Christ
as if he were a god." This is all that we know apart
from the mass of material found in the gospels.

This fact is not surprising since information about ancient figures comes largely through such sources. Jesus is no exception. We know of the Man of Nazareth from the "receivers"—people who responded to the impact of his personality. They felt compelled to find a place for him in their thoughts and in their lives. But they also felt obliged to interpret him. This is natural, and indeed inevitable. When someone has had an important experience, say, meeting a great states-man, he necessarily interprets that experience. It involves the person's understanding of the meeting and the conversation with the man, all of his previous thoughts about diplomacy, his earlier experiences with distinguished leaders, and any ideas he has about the subject. Most of the time, of course, people are not deeply conscious of this complex process of interpreta-tion. But sometimes, especially when the meeting and experience have been almost overwhelming, they recog-nize that their expectations and desires have played a part in making sense of what has happened to them.

So it was with Jesus. The way in which he was re-ceived inevitably colored the way in which he was re-membered. And the way in which he was received was very largely determined by what the receivers already thought and felt about God and men, about God's working in the world, about the meaning of their Jew-ish history, and about the expectation of the fulfill-ment of God's purpose.

In order to see how Jesus was received, we must look again at the gospels, this time to see what they reveal about the attitudes of the people who handed on the stories of Jesus. How did people at that time look at him? How did they think of him?

The general opinion about Jesus, as he traveled and spoke in Palestine, was that he was a surprising, new kind of rabbi or teacher. He did not appeal to traditional interpretations of the Torah, the sacred books of the Jew, but gave his own meanings to this ancient and accepted expression of the divine will. He spoke with authority. There was a forthright and definite quality in his sayings that greatly attracted the common people who "heard him gladly." It must have been refreshing for them to listen to a man who obviously knew what he was talking about and who had no hesitation in saying exactly what he thought. The gospels indicate that in the earlier days of his public ministry, people responded to him with strong enthusiasm, although later on, when he began to speak of "hard things, many no longer walked with him."

As we know, the accepted leaders of the Jewish nation were not impressed. They were accustomed to a more traditional kind of approach and perhaps they were also inclined to be jealous. They took a more critical attitude toward Jesus. After all, Jesus had not received the usual rabbinical training, and clearly that alone would have made the leaders critical of what he had to say.

Not only did Jesus seem a new kind of teacher, but he also "went about doing good." The Acts of the Apostles, in the New Testament, mentions that he "healed all manner of disease." Here was a man who seemed to possess remarkable healing powers. Unquestionably, there were many other Jews who were also able to help their fellowmen in this way, for there are occasional references in the gospels to healings by others. But Jesus always attributed this power to the power of God.

Jesus was a new kind of teacher, a remarkable healer, a good man who liked people, who was fond of children, and who welcomed women into his audience. This was unusual because women held a kind of second-class position among the Jews. But he was also taken to be a prophetic figure, a man who spoke for God. John the Baptizer had been recognized as a prophet, too, but Jesus had a more positive attitude and was not so severe and stern. Certainly, this kind of prophet would be "heard gladly," even if those who heard him did not always understand him.

People saw that Jesus cut deep into the superficiality of the current thinking about God and his people. They realized that his message showed the deepest sensitivity to the actual needs of men and women. For example, Jesus said "the Sabbath was made for man, not man for the Sabbath." He meant that human needs always took precedence over any observance, however hallowed. And when somebody got into an argument with him, Jesus was able to make very clear what was wrong with his opponent's thoughts. Usually he showed that people were so bound by their conventional ideas that they were unable to see the divine intention in the ancient Law. Sometimes these encounters were marked by humor, for Jesus was not always solemn and severe. People were a little afraid to engage in this sort of debate with him, for they found that they always came off second-best. This was certainly not a pleasant experience for religious leaders. So he was often rejected by the leaders as an irresponsible critic of accepted piety.

Some Jews regarded Jesus as one who would rally the people in their struggle for independence from the Romans. In modern times there has been much discussion of the relationship between Jesus and the Zealots, who were plotting the overthrow of the foreign rulers, probably by military means. The theory that Jesus was closely related with the Zealots has been much exaggerated, but there can be little doubt that some who received Jesus understood him in this way. It is even possible that Judas Iscariot himself, one of the intimate companions of Jesus, had assumed that eventually the prophet would head just such a revolt. Certainly this was one of the charges made against Jesus at his trial. But it is impossible to think that Jesus himself was a political revolutionary figure. The tenor of his teaching and the general quality of his actions do not bear out any such an idea.

It is not recognized often enough that Jesus was loved by many who heard him and most certainly by his most intimate companions. He was "received" as a friend, as well as a teacher, prophet, and healer. There was a simplicity and directness about him that matched the forthrightness and vigor of his speech. He did not seem hard to approach or difficult to get along with. He genuinely cared for people—or rather, he genuinely cared for the particular person with whom he was dealing. He gave the feeling that at a particular moment each person counted because Jesus was interested in him or her.

There is an old Christian song that speaks of Jesus as "the sinner's friend." The statement it makes is entirely true to the material we have about Jesus. Ordinary, erring, misguided men and women felt that they had found in Jesus someone who wanted to be, and who was, their genuine friend.

Within the circle of Jesus' immediate followers, the disciples, there were more profound feelings as to what and whom he represented. He was received by them in a deeper sort of way.

Certainly they, too, regarded him as a friend; he attracted and interested them. Otherwise they would never have been ready to "leave all and follow him" when he gave them the invitation to do so. The "little flock" referred to in Luke's Gospel was very close to him. They shared his daily life and were admitted to his innermost thoughts about God's purpose, the meaning of His kingdom, and the care that God had for each of His human children. The disciples had been with Jesus in good times and bad. They had been present when he was heard gladly and when he was rejected by the religious leaders. They knew of the times when he separated from them to engage in private prayer, and they were aware of the intimacy of his personal relationship with God.

The disciples also knew Jesus to be their teacher, who interpreted the deepest meaning of the ancient Law. What he said was for them plainly and simply the truth. They also undoubtedly understood him to be a prophet, the one who served as the mouthpiece for God in declaring the message that God wished them to hear.

It is not certain whether the disciples regarded Jesus as more than the greatest of the prophets, although the gospels give that impression. At Caesarea Philippi, it is said that Simon Peter called Jesus "the Messiah." However, it is not likely that this was, in fact, the moment when the disciples came to this conviction. It is much more likely that they believed this after the passion, crucifixion, and burial, when the disciples were

93

convinced that Jesus had "been seen by them" or had "appeared to them" triumphant over death.

The gospels make it plain that Jesus was not content to leave his disciples with the idea that the messiah would be worldly or majestic. The one who was the messiah must be rejected and killed. To the ordinary Jew, this was an absurd idea, and the disciples were quite ordinary Jews. When Jesus went up to Jerusalem with his companions, they did not expect that he would undergo the horrifying experiences that took place. Despite Jesus' warning, they expected that in some way he would overcome his enemies. But it did not happen that way. His enemies appeared to have won the victory.

After Jesus was buried, for a short time he was received, understood, and interpreted by his disciples as a failure. And since he himself had failed, his message and mission must also have been failures. Yet, strangely this notion of his failure did not persist for more than a very few days. Instead, the note of victory once again asserted itself. Within a short time the disciples were proclaiming "Jesus and the resurrection."It was then, with this strange conviction of Jesus' victory burning in their hearts, that they began to read the meaning of his whole life and teaching in the light of the Jewish expectation of a messiah. He had been victorious through defeat, triumphant in the very fact of his being rejected.

There is certainly a mystery about this. And there is a mystery about Jesus himself as he was received by those who knew him best. This is shown clearly several times in the gospels. For example, in Mark, the disciples were going up to Jerusalem with Jesus, and "Jesus was before them, and they were full of apprehension and they were afraid" (Mark 10:32). Again, there is the saying of Peter on one occasion, "Depart from me, for I am a sinful man, Lord" (Luke 5:8). The significance of this impression is given by Dr. Bethune-Baker in *The Christian Religion*, Volume I:

No account of what people thought about him in his lifetime is true unless it does justice to the evidence that, in spite of all his obvious humanity and intimate fellowship with them, they felt that there was more in him than they could grasp and understand, some unknown quantity or quality which, while it won them to him, yet at the same time baffled them and sometimes awed them and almost frightened them. The warm-hearted and hopeful friend could also be the stern and austere Master, who could be withering in denunciation and demanded the impossible from his friends and followers, though he said that it was not impossible but just what was to be—"Ye shall be perfect, even as your heavenly Father is perfect" (Matthew 5:48). There was a veil of mystery surrounding him, suggesting much more than met the eye or found expression in act and word.

It was to account for this mystery and suggestiveness, part of the actual experience of those who knew him in his lifetime in the world, as well as to account for all that he was and did after the Resurrection, that the later explanations and doctrine of the Church were developed.

The beginnings of that development are found in the gospels themselves. Mark's Gospel, for example, begins with the explicit statement that the material that it contains is the historical ground for "the good news of Jesus, the Messiah, the Son of God." As these words are used by the author of that gospel, it is plain that he means by "Son of God" something far more profound than is implied when any other man is called God's "son." For Mark, Jesus is God's son in a special and unique way, just as Mark's Gospel itself shows us how the idea of "messiah" came to be interpreted in terms of Jesus' suffering and death.

The final conclusion concerning the development of belief about Jesus may best be seen in the first chapter of John's Gospel:

In the beginning was the Word, and the Word was with God, and the Word was God. He was in the beginning with God; all things were made through him, and without him was not anything made that was made. In him was life, and the life was the light of men. The light shines in the darkness, and the darkness has not overcome it.

There was a man sent from God, whose name was John. He came for a testimony, to bear witness to the light, that all might believe through him. He was not the light, but came to bear witness to the light.

The true light that enlightens every man was coming into
the world. He was in the world, and the world was made
through him, yet the world knew him not. He came to his
own home, and his own people received him not. But to all
who received him, who believed in his name, he gave power
to become children of God; who were born, not of blood nor
of the will of the flesh nor of the will of man, but of God.

And the Word became flesh and dwelt among us, full of
grace and truth; and we have beheld his glory, glory as of
the only Son from the Father. John [the Baptist] bore witness to him, and cried, "This was he of whom I said 'He who
comes after me ranks before me, for he was before me.' "
And from his fullness have we all received, grace upon grace.
For the law was given through Moses; grace and truth came
through Jesus Christ. No man has ever seen God; the only
Son, who is in the bosom of the Father, he has made him
known.

The references to "the Word" probably have their
origin in certain Jewish ideas of God's "wisdom"
found in their religious history. God was thought to
have created the world "through His wisdom." God
was also thought to be utterly mysterious and in most
respects quite unknown, but again "through His
word" He had revealed something about Himself. By
the word, He disclosed "what He was up to in creation."

John's Gospel declares that this word of God is
genuinely divine. It has always been with God, and
wherever God is, there His word is. This same word has

always and everywhere been present in the creation, giving light to every man. This means that whatever is created, including human life itself, is grounded in and based upon God's outgoing activity. Wherever men have had a glimpse of truth, this has come to them through the same word of God. The word has always been present, but men have not responded to it as fully as they could and should. The Jewish people, above all, should have grasped its meaning, but John said they had rejected it.

We could say that John's great assertion is that Jesus is the place in history where the word of God is most completely and distinctively expressed in human terms. The word is, in fact, "God only begotten"; the word is the unique son of God and the unique son is manifested in the total life of Jesus. Through that life God himself, the ultimate mystery and meaning of all things, is now at last revealed to us.

This is the highest possible claim that anyone can make on behalf of the Man of Nazareth. John dares to assert that in Jesus, God has decisively acted in human history and in the affairs of men.

So Jesus was "received" in the early days of the first Christian century as friend, teacher, healer, prophet, messiah, and suffering servant. He was also received by the end of that century as the one in whom God was at work in His world, in human terms and in a real human life. Although the truth of that statement is a matter of Christian faith, it is important because it shows the way in which Jesus was given meaning by the early Christians.

The gospels show a gradual movement from straightforward recordings that describe Jesus as teacher and prophet, to profound religious interpretation of his unique significance. The seeds of this development are present in the first response of love and obedience made to Jesus in the days of his Palestinian ministry. This response led to further assertions, and the end of the process is to be found in the opening verses of John's Gospel in the New Testament. It is a development that can be clearly traced and must be taken into account in any attempt to assign Jesus his proper significance in the world. For in truth, we know about Jesus only by seeing him through the eyes of those who received him.

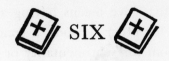

SIX

JESUS' ROLE
IN HISTORY

The name of Jesus is known throughout the world. For nearly two thousand years that name has signified for Christians the person and life of the one whom they worship and serve. And millions of non-Christians respect and admire Jesus as one of the greatest men who ever lived. This is why there is truth in the saying that sooner or later everybody must come to terms with the Man of Nazareth. It is appropriate, then, to discuss some of the ways in which his name and teachings have influenced mankind.

Jesus has taught men how they ought to live with one another. His teaching is essentially an insistence that love is what matters most in all human relationships. He ruled out once and for all the idea of re-

taliation—"an eye for an eye, a tooth for a tooth."
Jesus showed that love means having a genuine personal concern for other persons, a concern in which
there is no room for sentimentality or for judgment
based on superficial appearances. Love, for Jesus,
meant openness, willingness "to go the second mile,"
and penetration into the heart of the other. John's
Gospel says that Jesus "knew what was in man." He
seemed to get inside the lives of other people, seeing
them and loving them as they really were and not as
they seemed to be. For this reason, Jesus stressed the
supreme importance of one's attitude toward oneself
and others. He was aware of the deeper human desires under the surface emotions of people, and he
understood that only a genuine desire to be loving
would result in loving action toward others.

Millions of men and women have discovered that
this kind of love is the only possible basis of human
life. No matter how badly they have fallen short of
that ideal, they have recognized its necessity. Yet they
have come to know that only when men and women
have this kind of attitude, springing from the deep
desire to be in "love and charity with their neighbors,"
are they able to live together in peace and genuine
unity.

Jesus represents the standard or pattern for true
manhood. Many who entirely reject the Christian claim
that Jesus is the expression of God's nature still accept

the conviction that Jesus was what every man ought to be. As the ideal man, Jesus expressed a faithful surrender to, and a loving communion with, the deepest creative force in the universe. Jesus feared God, not as if he were frightened of Him, but because God was always to be reverenced and obeyed. He loved God, too, as a son loves his father. If Jesus was "the man for others," he was first and always "the man for God." That came first with him, as God must always be first for anyone who believes in Him. Jesus believed in God with the whole of his being.

There is no point in "imitating Jesus," if that means attempting to reproduce the particular things that he said or did. It would be absurd today to follow literally the precept that we are to "give to him that asketh of us." To do that, we would always have to give every beggar exactly what he requests. That would be the destruction of human society, and would fail to give that beggar the best assistance demanded of us. Jesus' admonition may be applied today in a different fashion, but with the same intention. We should see that the needy are given food, clothing, and shelter. By today's standards such assistance includes the use of welfare agencies, hospitals and clinics, or legal assistance. It may mean changing the laws so that people are protected from exploitation. But whatever the assistance, it demands a personal concern for the individual himself.

Since Jesus can be taken as a model of the supreme truth about man, he can provide an ideal toward which each of us can strive. Jesus has also been the main source in human history for the persisting conviction that God's quality or character, his inmost heart, is describable only by the word "love." "God is love," says one of the books in the New Testament. The writers came to this conviction from looking at what Jesus did and listening to what Jesus said. Jesus disclosed the nature of God as genuinely loving, truly concerned with His creation, and always giving Himself for His human children.

The unique thing about Jesus was that the impression he made was so vivid, the impact of his personality so strong, that there was no escaping his conviction. Since Jesus had lived, the only God whom men could acknowledge was a God who was like Jesus—that is, a God whose character was the same as that of the man Jesus. Even today, if anybody believes in God at all, he cannot accept a picture of God as sheer power or impersonal energy or as a cosmic drive. That would not be God, since Jesus came. To be God is to be one who is not only supreme over all things as their creator and their sustainer; it is also to be one who is worshipful. Men have discovered, since Jesus, that they cannot worship power or energy or drive. They can be afraid of these, they can cringe before them, they can fall down in sheer terror, but they cannot worship. Worship means that one adores, at the same time recognizing the perfection of the adored one, a perfection in whose presence one feels inadequate and imperfect.

The ordinary man and woman, in every part of the world where the name of Jesus has become familiar, may or may not "believe in God," but if there is any God in whom he believes and whom he is prepared to worship, it is "the God and Father of our Lord Jesus Christ." If there is a God at all, his nature, character, or quality of being is the self-giving love which Jesus embodied in his own life and declared in his teaching to be the truth about God and man.

Through Jesus, a relationship has been established between God and man which is full and free. This belief is held only by those who "profess and call themselves" by the name of Jesus Christ himself. For them, Jesus is the Savior who has brought atonement between God and man. Countless numbers of people feel that before they "met" Jesus Christ they were in some way alienated from God by their own choice and not because God wished it to be so. They have sensed their "sin." Sin is what separates men from God. It is not simply a failure to obey conventional moral standards or a matter of bad conscience, but a feeling that things between God and man are not as they should be. Such people have declared that in and through their meeting with Jesus their outlook has been changed. Now they feel "at one" with God. Now they have been given both the desire to fulfill God's will and some capacity to act as they desired.

Jesus has brought God and man together in a new and full unity, in which men find themselves free to live as God's children.

Finally, there is the deep belief in Jesus himself— not only in what he said and exemplified, but belief in him as a living man. To the Christian, Jesus was indeed a real man in every sense of the word. Yet there is more. "Jesus is that person in history in whom God acted with singular intensity and fullness, although the act was accomplished in a genuine human life which shared all the limitations and conditions of human experience." The traditional term for this belief is "the Incarnation," a word that means that in Jesus, God was "enfleshed." This does not imply that Jesus was God "with skin on." "Flesh" in Jewish thought signified the totality of human existence.

At every point in Christian history the answer to the question "What think ye of Christ?" has been, and still is, He is the "Word made flesh." He is the point and place in human affairs in which God, as He moves outward to express Himself, finds a vivid and unique instrument for His self-expression so far as men are concerned. The word "instrument" is the word that the great Christian thinker Athanasius used as long ago as the early years of the fourth century in attempting to explain what Jesus means to Christians. Athanasius called Jesus the *organon,* or instrument, for the Word of God, or God as He expresses Himself in His creation.

BOOKS FOR
FURTHER READING

1. For general guidance and help while reading the gospels, and also for informative articles on the background in Jewish history and thought:

The Interpreter's Bible, commentaries on Matthew, Mark, Luke, John. Nashville: Abingdon Press, 1960.

2. For following the cross-references and parallels in the first three gospels:

Gospel Parallels. New York: Thomas Nelson, 1949.

3. For assistance in understanding biblical ideas, as well as the physical setting of the biblical narratives, and other matterial, including the so-called Dead Sea Scrolls:

The Interpreter's Dictionary of the Bible. Nashville: Abingdon Press, 1962.

4. The best English text of the Bible is the *Revised Standard Version,* which exists in many editions.

5. For an explanation of the principles of New Testament criticism and a discussion of the various theories which have been, or are, held about the writing of the gospels:

Fuller, R. H. *A Critical Introduction to the New Testament*. London: Duckworth, 1966.

Grant, F. C. *The Growth of the Gospels*. Nashville: Abingdon Press, 1933.

6. For a discussion of these matters and also of Jesus' life and teaching:

Bethune-Baker, J. F. *Early Traditions about Jesus*. New York: Seabury Press, 1956.

7. For a sketch of "what Jesus did," as competent modern scholars present it:

Dibelius, Martin. *Jesus*. Philadelphia: Westminster Press, 1949.

Ferris, T. P. *The Story of Jesus*. New York: Harper, 1953. A beautiful, simple, but scholarly presentation.

Goquel, Maurice. *The Life of Jesus*. London: George Allen and Unwin, 1933.

Knox, John. *Jesus Lord and Christ*. New York: Harper, 1958. Perhaps the most useful and illuminating work in recent years, so far as "what Jesus did" is concerned.

8. For a sketch of "what Jesus said," by competent modern scholars:

Branscomb, B. H. *The Teachings of Jesus*. Nashville: Abingdon Press, 1931.

Davies, W. D. *The Sermon on the Mount*. Cambridge: Cambridge University Press, 1966.

Dibelius, Martin. *The Sermon on the Mount*. New York: Scribner, 1940.

Grant, F. C. *The Gospel of the Kingdom*. New York: Macmillan, 1940.

Manson, T. W. *The Teaching of Jesus*. Cambridge: Cambridge University Press, 1965.

9. For a discussion of Jesus' "miracles":

Richardson, Alan. *The Miracle Stories of the Gospels*. New York: Harper, n. d. A conservative discussion of the miracles reported in the four gospels.

Thompson, J. M. *Miracles of the New Testament*. London: Arnold, 1910. Out of print, hard to obtain, but in some libraries. The most thorough examination of all the miracle-stories from a "modernist" point of view.

10. For a consideration of "how Jesus was received" and what Christians have believed about him:

Bethune-Baker, J. F. *The Faith of the Apostles' Creed*. New York: Seabury Press, 1955.

Cadbury, H. J. *Jesus: What Manner of Man?* New York: Macmillan, 1947.

Knox, John. *Jesus Lord and Christ*. New York: Harper, 1958.

The author of this book has also written a large volume on Christian faith in Jesus, which starts with the kind of approach used in these pages and goes on to discuss how Jesus can be understood in modern terms:

The Word Incarnate. New York: Harper, 1959. While parts of this work are "difficult," since it was written for scholars, the reader may wish to see how the writer developed ideas included in the present book. The author has also written a shorter popular book:

Rethinking the Christian Message. New York: Seabury Press, 1956. In this work several chapters discuss points raised in the presentation in the present volume.

111

INDEX

113